200 recipes for kids

D0048940

hamlyn | **all colour cookbook**

200 recipes for kids

Emma Jane Frost

An Hachette UK Company
www.hachette.co.uk

First published in Great Britain in 2009 by Hamlyn,
a division of Octopus Publishing Group Ltd
2–4 Heron Quays, London E14 4JP
www.octopusbooks.co.uk

Copyright © Octopus Publishing Group Ltd 2009

Some of the recipes in this book have previously appeared in other books published by Hamlyn.

All rights reserved. No part of this work may be reproduced or utilized in any form or by any means, electronic or mechanical, including photocopying, recording or by any information storage and retrieval system, without the prior written permission of the publisher.

ISBN: 978-0-600-61929-1

A CIP catalogue record for this book is available from the British Library

Printed and bound in China

1 2 3 4 5 6 7 8 9 10

Both metric and imperial measurements have been given in all recipes. Use one set of measurements only, and not a mixture of both.

Standard level spoon measurements are used in all recipes.
1 tablespoon = one 15 ml spoon
1 teaspoon = one 5 ml spoon

Ovens should be preheated to the specified temperature – if using a fan-assisted oven, follow the manufacturer's instructions for adjusting the time and the temperature.

Fresh herbs should be used unless otherwise stated.

Medium eggs should be used unless otherwise stated.

Portion sizes are for the average adult and child aged around seven, so you will need to adjust portions according to the appetite and age of your child.

contents

introduction	6
breakfasts	14
inspired lunches	38
delicious dinners	76
on-the-run suppers	108
café alternatives	134
super snacks	154
desserts	194
fruity refreshers	220
index	236
acknowledgements	240

introduction

introduction

In our minds, mealtimes are a relaxing and happy affair. Children and parents eat together around the table, conversation is exchanged, and every plate is scraped clean. The reality of feeding a family is usually very different. There is often only one parent in the kitchen trying to keep the children entertained while preparing the meal, the main ingredient is often in the freezer when it should have been defrosted at least 24 hours previously, and one child needs to get to a swimming lesson! Because we would all love a more stress-free life, this book has been written to help make mealtimes less of a battle, more fun, more interesting – not to mention healthier and more successful for everybody involved.

Recipes for every occasion

As parents, we all know that children can be notoriously difficult to cook for. Many of us fall into the habit of cooking the same dishes over and over again, simply because we cannot bear the idea of scraping wasted food into the bin at the end of a meal. However, a child's formative years are when they learn to accept and like new foods, and it is therefore of great importance to encourage them to experiment with new tastes and different textures as often as you can.

This book has been put together with this in mind, but also with the knowledge that children are generally fussy creatures and like their food to be simple and to look good. Each recipe has been photographed to show you exactly what you will be cooking (and what they will be eating), and has of course been tested for child-appeal. To prevent your children getting bored by the same meals, we have also added a creative variation at the end of each recipe, giving you all the mealtime inspiration you should ever need for your family in one handy package!

Breakfast time

The first chapter gives you no fewer than 22 ideas for new breakfasts. Most children start the day with a bowl of shop-bought cereal, but remember that children's metabolism is

very high. Particularly for those children who are going to school, breakfast really is the most important meal of the day, in that it is designed to power them all the way through to lunchtime. A hungry stomach will lead to lack of concentration, and a lack of nutrients does not bode well for a good brain function, so fill them up in the morning with great food that they will love – fruit, seeds, oats, eggs and yogurt – and see what a difference it makes to their day.

Lunchtime

The next chapter, 'Inspired lunches', is designed to break you out of the cheese, tuna and ham sandwich rut that so many of us find ourselves in at lunchtime. Toddlers and youngsters of pre-school age are very often extremely hungry by midday, and a filling and nutritious meal is vital to ward off the grizzles later in the day.

Dinnertime

The 'Delicious dinners' you will find in the next chapter are exactly that – tried and trusted meals that kids will always eat and you will love. Some of these recipes may involve a little more work than others, but they have been included because they go down well with nearly every child around the table. They are therefore a great choice not just for your own children but also for when you have visitors for tea and you need to cater for varying tastes. And remember, if your children eat well at dinnertime, bedtime will inevitably be a calmer and happier experience.

Portable meals

Eating meals in the car on the way back from sports training, or in the pushchair on the way to pick up siblings from school, is unfortunately systematic of today's busy lifestyles. The 'On-the-run suppers' chapter is designed to take some of the stress out of those particularly busy days when a meal around the dining table really is impossible. The theory is that these recipes should be portable and fairly mess-free to eat in the car, pushchair or the leisure centre, but do remember your kitchen foil, clingfilm and baby wipes because spillages will undoubtedly occur.

Eating out

The chapter called 'Café alternatives' has been included because, like adults, most children like the idea of being treated to a meal out. These ideas are for when the budget does not stretch to a real café meal or for when time (or toddlers) don't allow for painful waits in understaffed restaurants. If you have the time and inclination, you can make these meals even more fun by setting the table in a different room, on a rug on the floor or outside in the garden to give everybody a change from the norm. Better still, keep in stock a selection of cardboard, party-sized, fold-out lunchboxes and serve your 'café' meal in these; you'll be surprised how much your child enjoys eating from a novelty container.

Nutritious snacks

'Snack', in some people's minds, is a dirty word. It conjures up images of additive-ridden chocolate bars and unnecessary, fattening treats. Actually, children invariably need nutritional snacks in between their three meals a day to keep their energy levels up and prevent attacks of bad behaviour. You will find that a lot of the recipes in the 'Super snacks' chapter are full of nutritious treats – vitamin-packed fruit, a selection of nuts and seeds (an excellent, portable form of protein), and an array of wholegrains to sustain energy.

Desserts

'Pudding' is sometimes regarded as an old-fashioned concept and has connotations of being stodgy and tasteless, but there is always a time and a place for spoiling children with a home-cooked, filling and nutritional dessert. Nearly all children love the taste of sugar, so when better to introduce them to new fruits and exotic tastes than with their dessert? Try the recipes in this chapter and watch your children wolf down raw and cooked fruit mixed in with crumble toppings, pancakes, chocolate, ice cream and tasty homemade custard.

The time factor

Feeding children, whether aged 2 or 12, can take time, so all the recipes in this book have been written with speed and ease in mind. At first, the recipes may take a little longer to prepare than you expect, and, if you have got stuck in the 'fish fingers and spaghetti bolognaise' rut, learning to use new ingredients will take a little time. The key to preparing successful meals for children is planning. This book provides a whole array of inspiring recipe ideas for breakfasts, lunches, dinners and snacks, so do try to find a few minutes (difficult though it may seem with a house full of demanding children) to plan your week's meals, buying only what you need for the recipes and defrosting meat and fish in plenty of time.

It is more important than ever when cooking for children that you have the staples to hand in your storecupboard, so always ensure your kitchen is stocked with the key ingredients that make great children's meals – soy sauce, plain flour, dried pasta shapes, Cheddar and Parmesan cheese, chicken stock cubes, tomato purée, olive oil, coconut milk, cinnamon, nutmeg and other herbs and spices. It is also wise to keep some nutrient-dense vegetables in the freezer to add into kids' meals – frozen spinach, sweetcorn and peas are usually great favourites. Don't forget, either, to have a spare can of tomatoes and some cans of salmon or tuna always at hand to help you whiz up a last-minute wonder.

Getting children involved

It may seem a bit of a cliché, but getting your children involved in the preparation of their food will almost certainly help their acceptance of it at the dinner table. Helping to prepare the meal will bring food into a child's imagination, and they can start to see it as an exciting part of their day. For this reason, many of the recipes in this book have been written with your child's participation in mind, no matter what their age or ability.

For instance, the Asparagus in Blankets recipe on pages 58–59 is great for encouraging children to try asparagus for the first time. Encourage them to roll the spears in Parma ham and let them sprinkle the Parmesan cheese over the top – young children will love 'peeping' the asparagus out through the tunnels. Alternatively, get them involved with chopping and sprinkling the ham and olives on top of the Mini Scone Pizzas on pages 118–119. Many children love watching the whizzing-up of the Breakfast Smoothies on pages 32–33 – but beware, as the noise of the blender may make younger children run from the room.

Growing your own ingredients

Taking this concept a stage further, parents of children who refuse to eat fruit and vegetables could benefit from getting out in the garden and growing some easy garden produce. Growing carrots from seed in large plastic tubs, for example, is a hugely rewarding experience for a child, particularly when they get to dig up the carrots and crunch them with the green tops still on.

For those with good intentions but no outdoor space, simply sprouting seeds on a windowsill can offer great benefits to your child's diet. Sprouted seeds are packed full of nutrients, and most children will love growing them and then sprinkling them over pasta or baked potatoes. Growing herbs such as thyme, parsley and mint in windowboxes is also a great way to get additional vitamins into your kids' meals – their job can be to pick the herbs, chop them and stir them into their own meals. This gives them a sense of ownership over the meal and helps them to feel in control of their food.

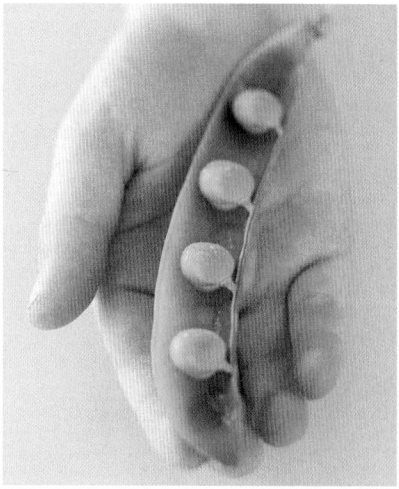

Choosing ingredients

When you are buying the ingredients for the recipes in this book, try to buy the freshest ingredients you can – fruit and vegetables start to lose their nutrients the moment they are picked, so the quicker you eat them after picking the more beneficial they are for your child.

Depending on your budget, you may also consider using organic ingredients. More and more people are choosing organic foodstuffs for their family, and it is easy to see why. Organic food has more beneficial minerals, essential amino acids and vitamins than non-organic food. Organic milk, for instance, has nearly 70% more essential fatty acid omega-3 than its non-organic equivalent. Organic meat is free from pesticides, chemicals and antibiotics, and organic crops are grown naturally and not routinely sprayed with pesticides. Although many of these pesticides are probably harmless, scientific tests are still being done to discover if there are any lasting negative effects on our health; until we know the outcome, it is worth buying organic foods to benefit our children with the additional nutrients they contain.

Portions and eating together

Most of the recipes in this book have been worked out based on a family of four – two adults and two children aged around seven – eating together. Obviously, if you are only catering for yourself plus one or two youngsters, it may be wise to halve the ingredients or, if the recipe allows, cook the whole amount and freeze a couple of portions for another day.

Whenever possible, however, it is recommended that you take the time to sit and eat with your children, for two main reasons. First, you are a role model for your kids, so if they see you eating a new food they are more likely to try it themselves. Second, mealtimes should be a social occasion, a time to talk and laugh and generally catch up with the day's activities. With today's busy lifestyles – working parents, after-school clubs and single parenting – it is rare for a parent to find the time to sit down and just talk with their children. Whenever possible, try to take time over a meal, particularly those meals where you are introducing new foods, and remember to praise a child who tries a new food, even if it is only a taste.

Get cooking!

A successful meal takes a bit of planning, a little time, some good ingredients, a dash of inspiration and some gentle encouragement. If cooking for your children has to date been a disappointing experience, this book should provide you with plenty of inspiration to turn the tide on those mealtime battles.

breakfasts

hot peach & cinnamon pancakes

Makes **8**
Preparation time **10 minutes**
Cooking time **20 minutes**

3 small ripe **peaches**
1 teaspoon **ground cinnamon**
6 tablespoons **maple syrup**
125 g (4 oz) **self-raising flour**
2 tablespoons **golden caster sugar**
1 **egg**
150 ml (¼ pint) **milk**
little **oil**, for greasing

Halve and stone the peaches. Roughly chop 1 of them and set it aside, then cut the remaining 2 into wedges and toss with a small pinch of the ground cinnamon and all the maple syrup in a small bowl and set aside.

Sift the flour and remaining cinnamon into a bowl and add the caster sugar. Make a well in the centre and set aside. Beat the egg and milk together well in a jug, then pour into the centre of the flour mixture. Mix quickly and as lightly as possible to make a batter the consistency of thick cream. Stir in the chopped peaches.

Lightly oil a heavy-based frying pan or flat griddle pan. Drop heaped tablespoons of the batter on to the pan surface and cook over a steady, moderate heat for 1–2 minutes until bubbles rise to the surface and burst. Turn the pancake over and cook for a further 1–2 minutes. Remove from the pan and keep warm while making the remaining pancakes.

Serve the pancakes warm, with a large spoonful of the peach and maple syrup mixture over the top of each.

For creamy banana pancakes, make the batter as above, replacing the peaches with 1 small banana, roughly chopped. Cook for 1 minute on each side until golden, and serve with 1 thinly sliced banana tossed with 2 tablespoons maple syrup over the top.

toffee-apple porridge

Serves **4**
Preparation time **10 minutes**
Cooking time **15 minutes**

500 g (1 lb) **eating apples**, peeled, cored and roughly chopped
½ teaspoon **ground mixed spice**
½ teaspoon **ground ginger**
5 tablespoons **soft brown sugar**
8 tablespoons **water**
600 ml (1 pint) **milk**
150 g (5 oz) **porridge oats**

Place the apples in a medium, heavy-based saucepan with the spices, 3 tablespoons of the sugar and the measured water. Bring to the boil, then reduce the heat to a simmer. Cover and simmer over a very gentle heat for 4–5 minutes, stirring occasionally, until the apples are soft yet still retaining some of their shape. Set aside with a lid to keep warm while making the porridge.

Bring the milk and remaining sugar to the boil, stirring occasionally. Remove from the heat and add the porridge oats. Stir well, then return to a low heat, stirring continuously for 4–5 minutes until the porridge has thickened.

Stir half the apple mixture through the porridge until well mixed, then ladle into 4 warmed serving bowls. Spoon over the remaining apple mixture and drizzle with the toffee apple syrup to serve, if liked.

For hot-pink, swirled porridge, mash 250 g (8 oz) fresh raspberries with 1 teaspoon golden caster sugar. Make up the porridge following the method above, then remove from the heat and spoon in the mashed raspberries. Using 1–2 stirs only, swirl the raspberries into the porridge, then ladle the swirled porridge into warmed bowls and serve with spoonfuls of Greek yogurt on top, if liked.

late great breakfast

Serves **4**
Preparation time **15 minutes**
Cooking time **15–20 minutes**

400 g (13 oz) sheet ready-rolled **puff pastry**
1 **red pepper**, cored, deseeded and roughly chopped
2 **tomatoes**, cut into wedges
125 g (4 oz) **button mushrooms**, cut in half
2 tablespoons **olive oil**
6 **eggs**
8 thin-cut rindless rashers **streaky** or **back bacon**
15 g (½ oz) **butter**, plus extra for greasing

Unroll the pastry and cut out four 12 x 10 cm (5 x 4 inch) rectangles. Using the tip of a small knife, make a shallow cut about 1 cm (½ inch) in from the edges of each rectangle, making sure you don't cut right through to the base. Place the pastry rectangles on a greased baking sheet.

Arrange the pepper, tomatoes and mushrooms on the pastry cases, keeping them away from the marked rims. Drizzle with 1 tablespoon of the oil and bake in a preheated oven, 220°C (425°F), Gas Mark 7, for 15–20 minutes until the pastry is well risen and golden.

While the pastry cases are baking, beat the eggs in a bowl. Heat the remaining oil in a frying pan and gently fry the bacon for about 2 minutes on each side until crisp, turning the rashers with a fish slice or wooden spatula. Melt the butter in a large saucepan. Tip in the beaten eggs and cook over a gentle heat, stirring continuously until scrambled.

Remove the baking sheet from the oven and transfer the pastries to serving plates. Spoon some scrambled eggs on to the centre of each and top with the bacon rashers. Serve while still hot.

For sausage & tomato pasties, place 8 good-quality chipolata sausages under a hot grill and cook, turning, for 8–10 minutes until golden and cooked, adding 8 halved, small tomatoes to the grill pan cut side up for the final 5 minutes of cooking. Halve the sausages and toss with the tomatoes and 1 tablespoon chopped parsley and use to fill the pastries, as above.

french toast with blueberries

Serves **4**
Preparation time **5 minutes**
Cooking time **10 minutes**

2 **eggs**
25 g (1 oz) **caster sugar**
½ teaspoon **ground cinnamon**
4 tablespoons **milk**
25 g (1 oz) **butter**
4 thick slices **brioche**
100 g (3½ oz) **blueberries**
8 tablespoons thick **Greek yogurt**
4 teaspoons **honey**, to drizzle

Beat the eggs in a bowl with the sugar, cinnamon and milk. Heat the butter in a large, heavy-based frying pan. Dip the brioche slices, 2 at a time, into the egg mixture on both sides, then lift into the hot pan and fry for 1–2 minutes on each side until golden.

Repeat with the remaining brioche slices. Mix half the blueberries into the yogurt.

Serve the warm French toasts with spoonfuls of the yogurt on top, the remaining blueberries scattered over and a thin drizzle of honey on top.

For sugar & cinnamon French toast, make the French toasts as above and place on serving plates once cooked and warm. Mix 50 g (2 oz) demerara sugar with ½ teaspoon ground cinnamon. Dredge each of the warm French toasts with the cinnamon sugar and serve.

herby beans & bacon

Serves **4**
Preparation time **10 minutes**
Cooking time **15 minutes**

1 tablespoon **olive oil**
6 rindless **streaky bacon** rashers, thickly chopped
1 small **carrot**, finely grated
400 g (13 oz) can **chopped tomatoes**
3 tablespoons **tomato purée**
2 tablespoons **clear honey**
400 g (13 oz) can **borlotti beans**, drained and rinsed
3 tablespoons chopped **flat leaf parsley** (optional)
4 thick slices **wholemeal** or **granary bread**
25 g (1 oz) freshly grated **Parmesan cheese** (optional)

Heat the oil in a large, heavy-based frying pan, then cook the bacon over a moderate heat for 2–3 minutes until beginning to turn pale golden. Add the carrot and cook for 1 minute more.

Add the tomatoes, tomato purée and honey and heat until the tomato juice is bubbling. Add the beans, then reduce the heat and simmer for 4 minutes, uncovered, until the tomato juice has reduced and thickened slightly. Stir in the parsley, if liked, and set aside.

Lightly toast the bread under a grill until golden and just crisp. Place on warmed serving plates and pile the herby beans and bacon on top. Sprinkle with the Parmesan, if liked.

For sausage & beans, cook 4 good-quality sausages in the oil for 5–6 minutes, turning until golden. Remove from the pan and slice, then return to the pan with 100 g (3½ oz) thinly sliced chorizo sausage and cook for 2 minutes, stirring occasionally until the sausages are golden. Continue as above and serve scattered with Parmesan, if liked.

morning muffins & tomato ketchup

Serves **4**
Preparation time **15 minutes**
Cooking time **20–25 minutes**

500 g (1 lb) good-quality **sausages**
1 tablespoon chopped **rosemary**
3 tablespoons chopped **parsley**
1 tablespoon **thick honey**
1 teaspoon **vinegar**
4 **eggs**
2 **English muffins**, halved

Ketchup
400 g (13 oz) can **chopped tomatoes**
2 tablespoons **maple syrup**
1 tablespoon **soft brown sugar**
3 tablespoons **red wine vinegar**

Place all the ketchup ingredients into a small, heavy-based frying pan and bring to the boil. Reduce the heat and gently simmer for 5–7 minutes, uncovered, stirring occasionally until the sauce is thick and pulpy. Whiz in a food processor until smooth, then place in a jar and cool. (Store in a refrigerator for up to 2 weeks.)

Cut along the length of each sausage, ease the skin off and discard it. Place the sausagemeat in a bowl with the herbs and honey and mix well. Using damp hands, shape into 8 small patties, then cook under a preheated medium grill for 10–12 minutes, turning once, until golden.

Meanwhile, bring a frying pan half-filled with water, with the vinegar added, to the boil. Reduce the heat to a simmer, then immediately break the eggs, well spaced apart, into the water and cook for 1 minute until the white is opaque. Remove from the water using a slotted spoon and keep warm.

Toast the muffin halves until golden and lightly crisp. Place a warm muffin half on to each of 4 serving plates and top with 2 sausage patties, a poached egg and a spoonful of ketchup.

For tomato & mushroom muffins, heat 1 tablespoon olive oil in a heavy-based frying pan and cook 250 g (8 oz) halved chestnut mushrooms and 4 halved plum tomatoes over a moderate heat for 4–5 minutes until soft and golden, turning occasionally. Poach the eggs and toast the muffins as above. Serve the muffins with the warm tomatoes, mushrooms and eggs on top with a drizzle of ketchup.

crunchy honey yogurt

Serves **6**
Preparation time **10 minutes**
Cooking time **5 minutes**

500 g (1 lb) **Greek yogurt**
125 g (4 oz) **strawberries**, quartered

Topping
50 g (2 oz) **flaked almonds**
50 g (2 oz) **pumpkin seeds**
50 g (2 oz) **sunflower seeds**
3 tablespoons **sesame seeds**
50 g (2 oz) **oats**
6 tablespoons **golden caster sugar**
4 tablespoons **clear honey**, plus extra to drizzle (optional)

Mix the almonds, seeds, oats and sugar in a large bowl. Line a large baking sheet with nonstick baking paper, then pour the nut and seed mixture over. Lightly shake the baking sheet to level the ingredients.

Drizzle the honey in thin streams over the top, then place under a preheated medium grill for 3–4 minutes until the sugar begins to caramelize and the nuts and seeds turn golden brown. Remove from the grill and set aside to cool and harden. Place the hardened nuts and seeds in a polythene bag and bash with a rolling pin to crush into a crunchy topping.

Spoon the yogurt into a bowl and fold in the strawberries. Divide between 6 serving bowls and sprinkle with the topping. (Store any leftover topping in an airtight container for up to 2 weeks.) Drizzle with more honey, if liked.

For yogurt-coated cereal topping, melt 125 g (4 oz) white chocolate in a heatproof bowl set over a pan of gently simmering water. Remove from the heat and add 2 tablespoons of natural yogurt. Crunch up 50 g (2 oz) cornflakes and 2 whole shredded wheat bicuits on to a baking parchment-lined baking sheet and scatter over 25 g (1 oz) rice puffs. Drizzle over the warm white chocolate and yogurt coating and refrigerate for 1 hour until set. Once set, transfer the paper to a chopping board and roughly chop the cereals to form a rough and chunky topping.

banana & choc wholemeal muffins

Makes **12**
Preparation time **15 minutes**
Cooking time **20–25 minutes**

150 g (5 oz) **self-raising wholemeal flour**
150 g (5 oz) **plain flour**
1 teaspoon **baking powder**
1 teaspoon **bicarbonate of soda**
½ teaspoon **salt**
125 g (4 oz) **golden caster sugar**
3 large ripe **bananas**, mashed
1 **egg**, beaten
75 ml (3 fl oz) **water**
75 ml (3 fl oz) **vegetable oil**
75 g (3 oz) **carob** or **plain dark chocolate**, roughly chopped

Sift the flours, baking powder, bicarbonate of soda and salt into a large bowl, then add the wheatgerm left in the sieve. Stir in the caster sugar. Mix together the bananas, egg, measured water and oil in a jug, then pour into the dry ingredients and gently mix until just combined. Fold in the carob or chocolate.

Line a 12-hole muffin tin with 12 paper muffin cases and three-quarters fill each with the mixture.

Bake in a preheated oven, 180°C (350°F), Gas Mark 4, for 20–25 minutes until they are well risen and spring back when you press them. Place on a wire rack to cool.

For fresh cherry & vanilla muffins, omit the bananas, mix 2 teaspoons vanilla extract into the egg, water and oil mixture, and fold in 250 g (8 oz) fresh pitted cherries instead of the chocolate. Bake as above.

breakfast smoothies

Serves **2**
Preparation time **5 minutes**

2 bananas
300 ml (½ pt) **milk**
4 tablespoons natural **fromage frais**
3 tablespoons **maple syrup**
50 g (2 oz) **hot oat cereal**

To serve
banana slices
malt loaf, cut into chunks

Place the bananas in a food processor with the milk, fromage frais and maple syrup and blend until smooth. Add the oat cereal and whiz again to thicken. Pour into 2 large glasses.

Arrange banana slices and chunks of malt loaf on 2 cocktail sticks and balance them across the top of the glasses, to serve.

For peanut-butter smoothies, replace the bananas with 4 tablespoons crunchy peanut butter, and change the maple syrup to honey. Make as above, whizzing until smooth.

breakfast crumble

Serves **8**
Preparation time **30 minutes**
Cooking time **45–50 minutes**

500 g (1 lb) **eating apples**, peeled, cored and roughly chopped
250 g (8 oz) **pears**, peeled, cored and roughly chopped
finely grated rind and juice of 1 **orange**
4 tablespoons **clear honey**
½ teaspoon **ground ginger**
175 g (6 oz) **strawberries**, hulled and quartered

Crumble
50 g (2 oz) **plain flour**
3 tablespoons **cold-milled flaxseed (ground linseed)**
50 g (2 oz) **butter**, cubed
50 g (2 oz) **porridge oats**
50 g (2 oz) **mixed seeds** (such as pumpkin, sunflower, sesame and hemp)
75 g (3 oz) **demerara sugar**

Place the apples and pears in a medium, heavy-based saucepan with the orange rind and juice, honey and ginger. Bring to a gentle simmer, stirring occasionally, then cover and simmer for 10 minutes until soft and slightly pulpy. Add the strawberries and cook for a further 2–3 minutes until soft, yet still retaining their shape. Remove the pan from the heat and transfer the mixture to an ovenproof gratin dish. Set aside while making the crumble.

Put the flour in a bowl and stir in the flaxseed. Add the butter and rub into the mixture until it resembles chunky breadcrumbs. Add the oats and again rub the fat into the mixture using your fingertips to distribute well. Stir in the seeds and sugar then sprinkle over the fruit.

Bake in a preheated oven, 200°C (400°F), Gas Mark 6, for 30–35 minutes until the topping is golden. Serve the crumble warm.

For amber crumble, omit the apples, pears and strawberries, roughly chop 4 ripe peaches and 6 ripe apricots and segment 4 oranges, then toss with 4 tablespoons clear honey and 1 teaspoon ground cinnamon. Place the uncooked fruit in the gratin dish, sprinkle with the crumble and bake as above.

melting mushrooms

Serves **4**
Preparation time **10 minutes**
Cooking time **9–12 minutes**

2 tablespoon **olive oil**
4 large flat **mushrooms**
4 small fresh **tomatoes**, roughly chopped
1 tablespoon **tomato purée**
4 tablespoons canned **cannellini beans**, drained and rinsed
1 tablespoon **clear honey**
1 tablespoon chopped **parsley**
50 g (2 oz) **Gruyère** or **Edam cheese**, thinly sliced
1 tablespoon freshly grated **Parmesan cheese**
4 slices **wholemeal toast**, to serve

Heat the oil in a large, heavy-based frying pan and cook the mushrooms over a moderate heat for 2–3 minutes, turning once, until they are softened. Place the mushrooms, stalk side up, on a foil-lined grill rack.

Add the tomatoes to the pan juices, and cook, stirring occasionally, for 4–5 minutes until the tomatoes are thick and pulpy. Add the tomato purée, beans and honey and continue to cook for a further 1 minute. Remove from the heat and stir in the parsley.

Divide the mixture between the mushrooms and arrange the slices of Gruyère or Edam over the top. Sprinkle the mushrooms with the Parmesan and place under a preheated hot grill for 2–3 minutes until golden and bubbling. Serve with slices of hot buttered wholemeal toast.

For egg-topped melting mushrooms, follow the recipe as above. Towards the end, poach 4 eggs in a frying pan half-filled with boiling water with 1 teaspoon vinegar for 1–2 minutes, then remove from the water using a slotted spoon and place on the mushrooms.

inspired lunches

traffic-light scrambled eggs

Serves **4**
Preparation time **10 minutes**
Cooking time **10 minutes**

3 tablespoons **olive oil**
1 small **onion**, finely chopped
½ **green pepper**, cored, deseeded and roughly chopped
½ **red pepper**, cored, deseeded and roughly chopped
½ **yellow pepper**, cored, deseeded and roughly chopped
1 **garlic** clove, crushed
3 tablespoons **water**
6 **eggs**, beaten
100 ml (3½ fl oz) **single cream**
4 thick slices **wholemeal bread**, to serve

Heat the oil in a large, nonstick frying pan and cook the onion and peppers over a moderate heat for about 4–5 minutes until softened. Add the garlic and cook for a further 1 minute, then add the measured water. Cover the pan and simmer for 2 minutes.

Beat together the eggs and cream in a jug. Remove the lid from the pan, pour in the eggs and stir over a low heat with a wooden spoon until the eggs are creamy and cooked.

Meanwhile, lightly toast the bread slices. Serve the eggs spooned over the warm toast.

For cheesy eggs & cress, beat together the eggs, cream and 50 g (2 oz) grated Cheddar cheese in a jug. Heat 15 g (½ oz) butter in a large nonstick frying pan and add the egg mixture. Stir over a low heat with a wooden spoon until creamy and cooked. Serve on warm wholemeal toast with freshly cut cress sprinkled over.

hummus pitta pockets

Serves **6**
Preparation time **15 minutes**
Cooking time **3 minutes**

400 g (13 oz) can **chickpeas**, drained and rinsed
3 tablespoons **tahini paste**
finely grated rind and juice of ½ **lemon**
1 tablespoon **olive oil**
3 tablespoons chopped **chives** (optional)
4 tablespoons **water**
2 medium **carrots**, grated
½ **cucumber**, chopped
handful of freshly cut **cress**
4 wholemeal or white **pitta breads**

Place the chickpeas in a food processor with the tahini paste and whiz until thick. Add the lemon rind and juice, olive oil, chives and measured water. Whiz again until smooth and creamy.

Toss the carrots, cucumber and cress in a bowl.

Lightly toast the pitta breads for 1 minute in a toaster until warm and slightly 'puffed'. Halve each pitta and fill, while warm, with the hummus and salad. Serve straight away.

For pockets with beetroot hummus, place 175 g (6 oz) cooked, drained beetroot (not in vinegar) into a food processor with 2 tablespoons tahini paste, the juice of ½ lemon and 1 teaspoon horseradish sauce. Whiz until smooth and creamy. Use to fill the pitta pockets as above, with the salad.

jewelled couscous

Serves **2–3**
Preparation time **20 minutes**
Cooking time **2 minutes**

150 g (5 oz) **couscous**
200 ml (7 fl oz) hot **vegetable stock**
50 g (2 oz) **green beans**, trimmed and cut into 1 cm (½ inch) lengths
1 small **orange**
2 tablespoons **olive oil**
1 tablespoon **clear honey**
1 **pomegranate**
½ small **pineapple**, chopped into small pieces
1 small **red pepper**, cored, deseeded and finely diced

Put the couscous in a heatproof bowl and add the stock. Cover and leave to stand for 20 minutes.

Meanwhile, bring a small pan of water to the boil and add the beans. Cook for 2 minutes. Drain the beans through a colander and rinse in cold water.

Finely grate half the rind of the orange and mix it in a small bowl with 3 tablespoons of orange juice, the oil and the honey. Whisk lightly with a fork.

Cut the pomegranate in half. Pull the fruit apart with your hands and ease out the clusters of seeds. Separate the seeds, discarding any white parts of the fruit, which are bitter. Add the pomegranate seeds, beans, pineapple and red pepper to the couscous along with the orange and honey dressing. Mix well and chill in the refrigerator until ready to serve.

For chicken, pea & mint couscous, make the couscous as above and leave to stand. Replace all the above vegetables with 175 g (6 oz) cooked chicken, 125 g (4 oz) cooked peas and 3 tablespoons fresh chopped mint. Mix the rind and juice of half a lemon into a 200 ml (7 fl oz) pot of crème fraîche and serve spooned over the couscous.

cheesy red dip with breadsticks

Serves **4**
Preparation time **45 minutes**, plus resting
Cooking time **30–40 minutes**

500 g (1 lb) **plain flour**
½ teaspoon **salt**
1 teaspoon **sugar**
5 g (¼ oz) fast-action **dried yeast**
300 ml (½ pint) **warm water**
6 tablespoons **olive oil**
2 tablespoons **sesame seeds**
1 tablespoon **poppy seeds**

Dip
2 **red peppers**, cored, deseeded and quartered
2 **tomatoes**
1 tablespoon **olive oil**
1 tablespoon **balsamic vinegar**
200 g (7 oz) **soft cheese**
1 tablespoon chopped **thyme** (optional)

Sift the flour and salt into a large bowl and add the sugar and yeast. Stir in the measured warm water and 3 tablespoons of the oil. Mix well to form a smooth dough, then turn out on to a well-floured surface and knead for 10 minutes until smooth and elastic. Cover and allow to rest for 15 minutes before kneading again for a further 10 minutes. Return to the bowl, cover with clingfilm and allow to stand for 30 minutes.

Knead the dough again to knock out the air, then cut into 4 pieces. Cut each quarter into 4 pieces, then stretch and roll each piece to make a long breadstick shape. Brush a baking sheet with the remaining oil. Roll the breadsticks in the oil, then sprinkle half with the sesame seeds and half with the poppy seeds. Bake in a preheated oven, 180°C (350°F), Gas Mark 4, for 30 minutes until golden and crisp. Remove from the oven and allow to cool.

Meanwhile, place the peppers on a baking sheet with the tomatoes and drizzle with the oil. Roast for 30 minutes in the oven with the breadsticks. Remove and place in a polythene bag and allow to cool. Remove from the bag and peel away the skins and discard. Place in a food processor with all the cooking juices, vinegar, cheese and thyme, if using and whiz until well blended and rough-textured. Transfer to a serving bowl and serve with the breadsticks.

For creamy avocado dip, place 1 large quartered avocado in a food processor with the finely grated rind and juice of 1 lime, 100 g (4 oz) soft cheese and 2 tablespoons sweet chilli sauce and whiz until smooth. Serve with the breadsticks.

beef & asparagus bagels

Serves **2**
Preparation time **5 minutes**
Cooking time **2 minutes**

4 **asparagus spears**, each cut into three
40 g (1½ oz) **watercress**
1 tablespoon **low-fat mayonnaise**
1 teaspoon **Dijon mustard** (optional)
2 **multigrain bagels**
100 g (3½ oz) **cooked beef**, very thinly sliced

Put a pan of lightly salted water on to boil. Boil the asparagus, if fresh, briefly, for 30 seconds or so, then drain well and set aside. (Asparagus in jars does not need cooking.)

Remove the larger stalks from the watercress and chop it. Place the mayonnaise and mustard, if using, in a bowl and stir in the watercress.

Split the bagels in half and toast under a preheated grill. Spread the halves with the flavoured mayonnaise. Top with the beef and asparagus spears and wrap securely. The bagels can be refrigerated for 1–2 days.

For smoked salmon & asparagus bagels, replace the cooked beef with 125 g (4 oz) smoked salmon and replace the watercress used to flavour the mayonnaise with 1 teaspoon finely grated lemon zest. Toast the bagels as above and fill with the salmon, lemon mayonnaise and asparagus.

bean, coconut & spinach soup

Serves **4**
Preparation time **5 minutes**
Cooking time about **20 minutes**

1 tablespoon **olive oil**
1 **onion**, chopped
2 large **garlic cloves**, crushed
1 teaspoon **ground coriander**
2 x 400 g (13 oz) cans **mixed beans**, drained
400 g (13 oz) can **coconut milk**
150 ml (¼ pint) **vegetable stock**
250 g (8 oz) fresh **spinach**

Heat the oil in a large, heavy-based saucepan and cook the onion and garlic over a moderate heat for 3–4 minutes until softened. Add the coriander and beans and cook for 1 minute, then add the coconut milk and stock. Bring to the boil, then reduce the heat, cover and simmer for 10 minutes.

Add the spinach to the pan. Stir well and cook for a further 5 minutes.

Whiz the soup in a food processor in 2 batches until smooth, then ladle into warmed serving bowls and serve immediately.

For red lentil & bacon soup, heat 1 tablespoon olive oil and cook 1 chopped onion, 100 g (3½ oz) roughly chopped streaky bacon, 2 large carrots (cut into large chunks) and 1 crushed garlic clove for 3–4 minutes. Add 250 g (8 oz) red lentils, ½ teaspoon ground nutmeg and 900 ml (1½ pints) chicken stock and bring to the boil. Reduce the heat, cover and simmer for 40 minutes until the lentils are soft and cooked. Whiz the soup in a food processor in 2 batches until smooth.

sunset wedges & soured cream

Serves **6**
Preparation time **20 minutes**
Cooking time **30–35 minutes**

3 **sweet potatoes**, skins on
2 large **baking potatoes**, skins on
3 tablespoons **olive oil**
1 teaspoon **Cajun spice**
2 tablespoons chopped **parsley**

Dip
150 ml (¼ pt) **Greek yogurt**
4 tablespoons **soured cream**
4 tablespoons chopped **chives**
2 tablespoons freshly grated **Parmesan cheese**

Cut the sweet potatoes in half, then cut each half into 4 wedges and place in a large mixing bowl. Cut the baking potatoes in half, then cut each half into 6 thick wedges and place in the bowl. Drizzle over the olive oil, then toss well to coat all the potato wedges.

Transfer the potatoes to a large baking sheet or oven tray in a single layer. Sprinkle over the Cajun spice. Roast in a preheated oven, 200°C (400°F), Gas Mark 6, for 30–35 minutes until golden and cooked through. Turn on to a serving platter and sprinkle with the parsley.

Mix the yogurt, soured cream, chives and Parmesan in a small mixing bowl. Serve the dip with the warm potato wedges.

For creamy cucumber & garlic dip to serve as an alternative accompaniment, replace the chives and Parmesan with ¼ grated cucumber and 1 crushed garlic clove. Stir in 2 tablespoons freshly chopped mint and mix well. Serve the dip with the warm potato wedges.

tomato-garlic bread with ham

Serves **2**
Preparation time **10 minutes**

1 **garlic clove**, halved
4 slices **soft white bread**
2 **tomatoes**, 1 halved and 1 thinly sliced
150 g (5 oz) finely sliced **ham**
75 g (3 oz) **Manchego cheese**, sliced

Rub the cut faces of the garlic all over the bread, concentrating particularly on the crusts. Repeat with the tomato halves.

Sandwich the bread with the ham, cheese and sliced tomato. Halve and wrap securely. The sandwiches can be kept in the refrigerator for 1 day.

For tomato-garlic bread with salami & mozzarella, flavour the bread with the garlic and tomato as above and fill with 150 g (5 oz) finely sliced salami and 75 g (3 oz) mozzarella. Add 1 sliced tomato. Warm on a baking sheet in a preheated oven, 200°C (400°F), Gas Mark 6, for 10 minutes before serving warm, cut into triangles.

pan-fried chicken wraps

Serves **4**
Preparation time **15 minutes**
Cooking time **5 minutes**

2 tablespoons **olive oil**
3 boneless, skinless **chicken breasts**, about 150 g (5 oz) each, thinly sliced into strips
3 tablespoons **clear honey**
1 teaspoon **wholegrain mustard**
4 **soft flour tortillas**

Coleslaw
¼ small **white cabbage**, finely shredded
1 large **carrot**, grated
3 tablespoons **olive oil**
2 tablespoons **red wine vinegar**
1 teaspoon **Dijon mustard**
2 tablespoons chopped **parsley**

Make the coleslaw. Put the white cabbage in a large mixing bowl with the carrot and toss together well. In a small jug whisk together the oil, vinegar and mustard. Pour over the cabbage and carrot and toss well to coat. Add the parsley and toss again. Set aside.

Heat the oil in a large nonstick frying pan and cook the chicken strips over a high heat for 4–5 minutes until golden and cooked through. Remove from the heat and add the honey and mustard. Toss well to coat.

Warm the tortillas in a microwave for 10 seconds on high (or in a warm oven), then spread each with the coleslaw and top with the chicken pieces. Wrap each tightly, then cut in half to serve.

For maple-glazed gammon wraps, omit the chicken and cut 3 x 175 g (6 oz) gammon steaks into strips. Heat the oil and cook the gammon over a high heat for 3–4 minutes until golden and cooked through. Remove from the heat and toss with 3 tablespoons maple syrup (instead of the honey) and the mustard. Assemble the wraps as above.

asparagus in blankets

Serves **4**
Preparation time **10 minutes**
Cooking time **15 minutes**

2 bunches thick **asparagus spears**, trimmed to about 15 cm (6 inches) long
1 tablespoon **olive oil**
25 g (1 oz) **butter**, softened
16 slices **Parma, prosciutto** or **serrano ham**
4 tablespoons freshly grated **Parmesan cheese**

Bring a large pan of water to the boil. Cook the asparagus for 5 minutes in the boiling water, then remove with a slotted spoon and place in a bowl. Toss with the olive oil.

Grease a gratin dish with the butter. Wrap each of the asparagus spears in a piece of ham and place them in the greased dish side by side. Sprinkle with the Parmesan and bake in a preheated oven, 200°C (400°F), Gas Mark 6, for 10 minutes until the cheese is golden and melted.

Serve the asparagus in blankets with chunks of warm fresh bread and homemade tomato ketchup (see pages 26–27).

For cheesy pizza-style asparagus, replace the Parma, prosciutto or serrano ham with thin slices of honey-roast ham and place the wrapped asparagus in the gratin dish. Sprinkle with 50 g (2 oz) chopped black olives and 100 g (4 oz) grated mozzarella instead of the Parmesan, and bake as above. Serve the pizza-style asparagus with garlic bread.

beanfeast

Serves **4**
Preparation time **10 minutes**
Cooking time **about 15 minutes**

200 g (7 oz) **tomatoes**
1 tablespoon **vegetable oil**
½ small **onion**, chopped into small pieces
1 **celery stick**, chopped into small pieces
2 x 300 g (10 oz) cans **haricot** or **cannellini beans**, drained and rinsed
2 teaspoons **wholegrain mustard**
2 tablespoons **black treacle**
3 tablespoons **tomato ketchup**
1 tablespoon **Worcestershire sauce**
4 slices **toast** or 4 **jacket potatoes**, to serve

Put the tomatoes into a heatproof bowl and just cover with freshly boiled water. Leave to stand for 1–2 minutes until the skins start to split. Carefully pour off the hot water and peel away the skins. Roughly chop the tomatoes on a chopping board.

Heat the oil in a medium, heavy-based saucepan for 1 minute. Add the onion and celery and fry gently for 5 minutes, stirring until just beginning to colour.

Tip in the beans, tomatoes, mustard, treacle, ketchup and Worcestershire sauce and stir the ingredients together. Heat until the liquid starts to bubble around the edges. Reduce the heat to its lowest setting and cover the pan with a lid. Cook gently for about 10 minutes until the tomatoes have softened to make a sauce.

Serve with toast or on jacket potatoes.

For lentil & paneer feast, replace the cans of beans with a 400 g (13 oz) can puy lentils, drained and rinsed and add to the pan with the tomatoes. Cook for 10 minutes, adding 250 g (8 oz) cubed paneer cheese for the final 2–3 minutes.

chinese-style turkey wraps

Serves **2**
Preparation time **10 minutes**
Cooking time **1–2 minutes**

½ teaspoon **vegetable oil**
100 g (3½ oz) **turkey breast**, thinly sliced
1 tablespoon **clear honey**
2 tablespoons **soy sauce**
1 tablespoon **sesame oil**
2 **soft flour tortillas**
50 g (2 oz) **bean sprouts**
¼ **red pepper**, cored, deseeded and thinly sliced
¼ **onion**, thinly sliced
25 g (1 oz) **mangetouts**, sliced
2 **baby sweetcorn**, thinly sliced

Heat the oil in a frying pan over a moderate heat and add the turkey to the pan. Stir for 1–2 minutes until cooked through. Reduce the heat and stir in the honey, soy sauce and sesame oil, making sure that the turkey is well coated. Set aside to cool.

Assemble a wrap by placing half the turkey mixture down the centre of a tortilla. Add half the bean sprouts and pepper, onion, mangetouts and baby sweetcorn. Repeat with the other tortilla. (Alternatively, retain the remaining tortilla and mixture for use another day; the mixture will keep for up to 24 hours in the refrigerator.)

Roll up the tortilla securely and wrap in nonstick baking paper (clingfilm can make the wrap rather soggy).

For Chinese-style pork & pak choi wraps, replace the turkey with 125 g (4 oz) tenderloin pork strips tossed with ½ teaspoon Chinese five spice and cook as above for 3–4 minutes. Add 1 small head pak choi, shredded with the honey, soy sauce and sesame oil and cook for a further 2 minutes. Assemble as above with 125 g (4 oz) beansprouts, omitting the mangetouts, onion and sweetcorn.

warm seedy rolls

Makes **12**
Preparation time **1 hour 40 minutes**, including resting time
Cooking time **15–20 minutes**

5 g (¼ oz) active **dried yeast**
300 ml (½ pint) **warm water** (not hot)
500 g (1 lb) **strong plain flour**, plus extra for dusting
1 teaspoon **salt**, plus a pinch
25 g (1 oz) **butter**, cut into cubes, plus extra for greasing
4 tablespoons **sunflower seeds**
2 tablespoons **poppy seeds**
2 tablespoons **pumpkin seeds**
1 **egg yolk**
1 tablespoon **water**

Sprinkle the yeast over the measured warm water, stir well and set aside for 10 minutes until it goes frothy. Sift the flour and salt into a large bowl and add the butter. Rub the butter into the flour until the mixture resembles fine breadcrumbs. Add all the seeds and stir. Make a well in the centre and add the yeast mixture. Stir well with a wooden spoon, then use your hands to mix to a firm dough.

Knead for 5 minutes until the dough feels firm, elastic and no longer sticky. Return to the bowl, cover with clingfilm and set aside in a warm place for 30 minutes until the dough has doubled in size.

Turn out the dough and knead again to knock out the air, then divide into 12 pieces. Knead each piece briefly, then form into a roll shape, or roll each piece into a long sausage shape and form into a loose knot. Place the rolls on a lightly greased baking sheet, cover with a clean tea towel and set aside in a warm place for 30 minutes until almost doubled in size.

Mix the egg yolk in a small bowl with a pinch of salt and the measured water and brush over the rolls to glaze. Bake in a preheated oven, 200°C (400°F), Gas Mark 6, for 15–20 minutes until golden and sounding hollow when tapped lightly on the base. Remove from the oven and allow to cool a little. Serve warm with soup.

For cheesy onion rolls, replace the seeds with 5 spring onions, very finely chopped and lightly cooked for just 1 minute in 1 tablespoon olive oil. Once glazed, sprinkle with 3 tablespoons freshly grated Parmesan cheese.

roasted vegetable couscous

Serves **6**
Preparation time **15 minutes**, plus soaking
Cooking time **30–35 minutes**

175 g (6 oz) **couscous**
1 **chicken stock cube**
450 ml (¾ pint) **hot water**
2 **courgettes**, cut into chunks
1 **red pepper**, cored, deseeded and cut into chunks
1 **yellow pepper**, cored, deseeded and cut into chunks
375 g (12 oz) **butternut squash**, peeled, deseeded and cut into chunks
1 **red onion**, chopped
5 tablespoons **olive oil**
3 tablespoons chopped **parsley** or **basil**
5 tablespoons **pine nuts**, toasted

Place the couscous in a bowl, crumble in the stock cube and stir well. Add the measured water, stir, then cover and set aside, while preparing and cooking the vegetables, to soak and swell.

Put all the prepared vegetables into a large roasting tin and drizzle over 3 tablespoons of the oil and toss to coat lightly. Roast in a preheated oven, 200°C (400°F), Gas Mark 6, for 30–35 minutes until the vegetables are soft and lightly charred.

Lightly fork the soaked couscous to fluff it up, then drizzle over the remaining oil and toss well. Add the warm vegetables, parsley or basil and pine nuts and toss well before serving.

For roasted vegetable quinoa with toasted cashews, replace the couscous with quinoa. Wash 175 g (6 oz) quinoa in a sieve, then drain. Place in a large, heavy-based nonstick frying pan and lightly toast over a moderate heat for 2–3 minutes until the grain turns a shade darker. Add 450 ml (¾ pint) water and 1 chicken stock cube and cook over a moderate heat for 8–10 minutes until the grain is tender and cooked. Drain and set aside. Add the roasted vegetables and parsley as above and replace the pine nuts with 100 g (4 oz) roughly chopped toasted cashews.

peking wraps

Serves **2**
Preparation time **10 minutes**
Cooking time **about 10 minutes**

1 **duck breast**, weighing about 175 g (6 oz), with skin, cut across into very thin slices
½ teaspoon **Chinese 5-spice powder**
1 tablespoon **vegetable oil**
2 large **soft flour tortillas**
2 tablespoons **hoisin sauce**
2 **iceberg lettuce leaves**, thinly shredded
5 cm (2 inch) piece **cucumber**, sliced into matchstick-sized pieces
2 **spring onions**, thinly sliced diagonally

Put the slices of duck on a plate and sprinkle with the 5-spice powder. Turn the slices in the spice until coated all over. Heat the oil in a small frying pan for 1 minute. Add the duck and fry gently for 5 minutes, turning the pieces with a fish slice. Using the fish slice, transfer the duck to a plate and leave to cool while you prepare the filling.

Heat the tortillas one at a time in the microwave on full power for 8 seconds. Alternatively, warm them under a hot grill or in a frying pan for approximately 10 seconds.

Spread the hoisin sauce over one side of each tortilla. Scatter a line of lettuce, then the cucumber, spring onions and duck down the centre of each tortilla, keeping the ingredients away from the ends.

Fold 2 sides of each tortilla over the ends of the filling, then roll them up tightly from an unfolded side so that the filling is completely enclosed. Cut the wraps in half, wrap in nonstick baking paper and chill in the refrigerator until ready to go.

For crispy lamb & lettuce Peking wraps, toss 175 g (6 oz) lamb fillet strips in the 5-spice powder and cook as above. Use shredded lettuce, spring onion and cucumber as before, as well as strips of finely sliced carrot.

tuna melts

Serves **2**
Preparation time **10 minutes**
Cooking time **11–13 minutes**

200 g (7 oz) can **tuna**, in oil or brine, drained
75 g (3 oz) frozen **sweetcorn**
3 tablespoons **mayonnaise**
2 **panini**, cut in half horizontally
75 g (3 oz) **Gruyère** or **Emmenthal cheese**, thinly sliced

Flake the tuna into a bowl. Put the sweetcorn in a small saucepan and pour boiling water over to just cover it. Cook for 3 minutes and drain through a sieve. Rinse the sweetcorn under cold water and add it to the tuna. Stir in the mayonnaise until well mixed.

Spread the tuna mixture over the two bread bases. Arrange the cheese on top of the tuna. Press the bread tops down firmly on the filling.

Heat a heavy-based frying pan or ridged grill pan for 2 minutes. Add the breads and cook on a gentle heat for 3–4 minutes on each side, turning them carefully with a fish slice or tongs. Wrap the tuna melts in nonstick baking paper and chill in the refridgerator until ready to serve.

For warm haloumi & vegetable melts, heat 1 tablespoon olive oil in a frying pan and cook 1 small, thinly sliced courgette and 1 thinly sliced red pepper for 3–4 minutes until softened. Fill the paninis with the vegetables and top with 125 g (4 oz) thinly sliced haloumi cheese. Cook as above, then transfer to serving plates and serve.

baked sweet potatoes & prawns

Serves **4**
Preparation time **10 minutes**
Cooking time **25–30 minutes**

1 tablespoon **olive oil**
4 large **sweet potatoes**, skin on, scrubbed, patted dry
250 g (8 oz) medium **prawns**, defrosted if frozen
1 ripe **avocado**, cut into small chunks
2 tablespoons **mayonnaise**
2 tablespoons **milk** or **water**
3 tablespoons **crème fraîche**
1 tablespoon **tomato purée**

To serve
ground paprika
1 small pot **sprouting alfalfa** (or other sprouting seeds)

Drizzle a little of the oil over each sweet potato, then rub it all over the skin. Put the potatoes on a baking sheet. Bake in a preheated oven, 200°C (400°F), Gas Mark 6, for 25–30 minutes until tender and cooked through.

Meanwhile, place the prawns and avocado in a bowl and toss together. Mix the mayonnaise with the milk or water until smooth, then add the crème fraîche and tomato purée and mix until well blended. Add the prawns and avocado and toss well to coat lightly.

Remove the sweet potatoes from the oven. Split the hot potatoes and fill them with the prawn mixture. Serve garnished with a pinch of paprika and some freshly cut sprouting seeds.

For baked sweet potatoes & creamy mushrooms, bake the sweet potatoes as above. Heat 1 tablespoon olive oil in a heavy-based frying pan and cook 250 g (8 oz) quartered chestnut mushrooms over a high heat for 3–4 minutes until golden and softened. Remove from the heat, add 200 ml (7 fl oz) crème fraîche and 1 teaspoon Dijon mustard and stir well for a few seconds until piping hot. Spoon into the sweet potatoes as above.

spicy chorizo wrap

Serves **2**
Preparation time **15 minutes**
Cooking time **5–7 minutes**

4 **eggs**
½ teaspoon **mild chilli powder**
50 g (2 oz) sliced **chorizo sausage**, cut into thin shreds
2 tablespoons **olive oil**
1 punnet **mustard and cress**
2 large **soft flour tortillas**
2 tablespoons **red pesto**

Break the eggs into a bowl and add the chilli powder. Whisk well until the eggs are completely broken up. Stir in the chorizo. Heat the oil in a small frying pan for 1 minute. Tip the egg mixture into the pan. When the eggs start to set around the edges, use a fork to push the cooked parts into the centre of the pan so the uncooked egg flows into the space. Keep doing this until the eggs are no longer runny, then let the omelette cook until just set (3–5 minutes). Slide the omelette on to a plate and leave to cool.

Cut the mustard and cress from the punnet and put it in a sieve. Rinse under cold water and leave to drain.

Prepare the tortillas by heating in the microwave on full power for 10 seconds. Alternatively, warm them under a hot grill or heat in the frying pan for approximately 10 seconds (wipe out the pan with kitchen paper first, taking care as it might still be hot).

Spread one side of each of the tortillas with the pesto and lay the omelette on top. Sprinkle with the mustard and cress. Roll up tightly so the filling is completely enclosed. Cut the wraps in half, wrap in nonstick baking paper and chill in the refrigerator until ready to serve.

For pesto chicken wraps, replace the chorizo with 75 g (3 oz) cooked and torn chicken pieces and 50g (2 oz) black olives, sliced. Spread the tortilla with 1 tablespoon green pesto and top with the omelette. Omit the mustard and cress, roll up and serve warm.

delicious dinners

green cheese pasta

Serves **4**
Preparation time **10 minutes**
Cooking time **10 minutes**

250 g (8 oz) **pasta shapes**
300 g (10 oz) fresh **spinach**
1 teaspoon **ground nutmeg**
50 g (2 oz) **butter**
50 g (2 oz) **plain flour**
600 ml (1 pint) **milk**
100 g (4 oz) **Cheddar cheese**, grated

Cook the pasta shapes for 8–10 minutes or according to packet instructions until just tender. Drain and set aside.

Meanwhile, place the spinach in a pan of boiling water and cook, stirring continuously, over a moderate heat for 2 minutes until wilted. Remove from the heat and drain well, then return to the pan and toss with the nutmeg. Set aside.

Melt the butter in a medium, heavy-based saucepan. Remove from the heat, add the flour and stir to form a thick paste. Return to the heat and cook gently for a few seconds, stirring continuously. Remove from the heat and gradually add the milk, stirring well after each addition. Return to the heat and bring to the boil, stirring continuously until the sauce has boiled and thickened.

Remove from the heat and add the spinach and cheese. Stir, then transfer to a food processor and whiz until smooth. Return to the pan and add the pasta. Stir well to coat, then divide between 4 warmed serving bowls.

For courgette & garlic pasta, replace the spinach with 3 large courgettes, trimmed and grated. Heat 1 tablespoon olive oil in a nonstick frying pan and cook the courgettes and 1 crushed garlic clove over a moderate heat for 4–5 minutes until soft and tender. Add 3 tablespoons of chopped chives, then add to the sauce in place of the spinach and whiz until smooth before tossing with the pasta.

chicken rice salad

Serves **4**
Preparation time **10 minutes**, plus cooling
Cooking time **about 15 minutes**

4 **chicken thighs**, skinned and boned
175 g (6 oz) **long-grain rice**
2 teaspoons **lemon juice**
2 tablespoons **peanut butter** (optional)
2 tablespoons **olive oil**
2 **pineapple rings**, chopped
1 **red pepper**, cored, deseeded and chopped
75 g (3 oz) **sugar snap peas**, sliced
4 tablespoons **peanuts** (optional)

Place the chicken thighs in a steamer set over boiling water for 10–12 minutes until cooked through. Alternatively, simmer them in shallow water in a frying pan for 10 minutes. Remove from the steamer or pan and set aside to cool.

Meanwhile, cook the rice according to the packet instructions. Drain and rinse under cold water to cool the rice completely, then tip it into a large bowl.

Make the dressing: mix together the lemon juice and peanut butter, if using, until well combined, then whisk in the oil.

Dice the chicken thighs into bite-sized pieces and stir into the rice. Add the pineapple, red pepper, sugar snap peas and peanuts, if using. Pour the dressing over the chicken rice salad and serve.

For prawn rice salad, make up the peanut dressing as above. Replace the chicken with 150 g (5 oz) prawns tossed with 2 tablespoons toasted sesame seeds. Cut ¼ cucumber into thin sticks and toss with the rice, peanut sauce, prawns and seeds.

salmon pasta bake

Serves **6**
Preparation time **20 minutes**
Cooking time **30 minutes**

250 g (8 oz) **pasta shapes**
25 g (1 oz) **butter**
25 g (1 oz) **plain flour**
300 ml (½ pint) **milk**
200 ml (7 fl oz) **crème fraîche**
100 g (4 oz) freshly grated **Parmesan cheese**
3 tablespoons chopped **herbs** (such as chives or dill)
2 x 200 g (7 oz) cans **red salmon**, drained and flaked
100 g (4 oz) frozen **peas**

Cook the pasta for 8–10 minutes or according to packet instructions until tender. Drain and set aside.

Heat the butter in a nonstick pan until melted. Remove from the heat, add the flour and stir well to form a thick paste. Return the pan to the heat and cook, stirring continuously, for 1 minute. Remove from the heat and gradually add the milk, a little at a time, stirring well until all the milk is used.

Return the pan to the heat and bring to the boil, stirring continuously until boiled and thickened. Add the crème fraîche and half the Parmesan and stir well. Add the drained pasta, herbs, flaked salmon and peas and toss gently to mix, taking care not to break up the fish. Transfer to 6 individual gratin dishes and sprinkle over the remaining Parmesan.

Bake in a preheated oven, 180°C (350°F), Gas Mark 4, for 20 minutes until golden and bubbling. Serve with warm bread and a simple salad.

For tuna pasta bake with sweetcorn, replace the salmon with 2 x 200 g (7 oz) cans of tuna in brine, drained and flaked, and replace the peas with 100 g (4 oz) sweetcorn. Add 1 tablespoon wholegrain mustard and mix well. Cut a garlic baguette into slices and place on top of the pasta. Sprinkle with the remaining Parmesan and bake as above until the bread is crisp and golden and the sauce is bubbling.

spaghetti bolognaise

Serves **6**
Preparation time **30 minutes**
Cooking time **35 minutes**

2 tablespoons **olive oil**
1 **onion**, finely chopped
2 **carrots**, grated
1 **courgette**, grated
500 g (1 lb) **lean beef mince**
2 tablespoons **plain flour**
2 tablespoons **tomato purée**
600 ml (1 pint) **rich beef stock**
200 g (7 oz) can **chopped tomatoes**
250 g (8 oz) **spaghetti** or **linguine**
freshly grated **Parmesan cheese**, to serve

Heat 1 tablespoon of the oil in a large, heavy-based saucepan and cook the onion, carrots and courgette over a moderate heat for 5–6 minutes, stirring occasionally until soft. Remove the vegetables from the pan and set aside.

Add the mince to the pan and cook over a high heat for 4–5 minutes, stirring frequently until browned all over. Return the vegetables to the pan, add the flour and stir well to coat lightly. Add the tomato purée to the beef stock and stir well, then add the stock to the meat along with the chopped tomatoes. Bring to the boil, then reduce the heat, cover with a lid and simmer for 20 minutes.

Meanwhile, cook the pasta for 8–10 minutes or according to packet instructions until tender. Drain and toss with the remaining oil. Arrange the pasta in warmed serving bowls and pile the bolognaise sauce on top. Sprinkle with the Parmesan.

For bolognaise pasta bake, cook 250 g (8 oz) macaroni until just tender. Drain and toss with 1 tablespoon olive oil. Make up the bolognaise sauce as above and mix with the macaroni. Transfer to a large gratin dish. Mix 200 ml (7 fl oz) crème fraîche with 3 tablespoons freshly grated Parmesan cheese and 2 tablespoons chopped parsley, and spoon over the top of the macaroni. Bake in a preheated oven, 200°C (400°F), Gas Mark 6, for 20–25 minutes until the topping is golden and bubbling.

potato & cheese röstis

Makes **4**
Preparation time **10 minutes**
Cooking time **25 minutes**

500 g (1 lb) **red** or **waxy potatoes**, unpeeled
50 g (2 oz) **mild Cheddar cheese**, grated
1 **red onion**, finely chopped
3 tablespoons **vegetable oil**
Tomato Ketchup (see pages 26–27), to serve

Put the potatoes in a large pan of water and bring to the boil. Boil for about 20 minutes until the potatoes are just cooked but firm. Drain and cool.

Peel the potatoes and grate them into a bowl. Stir in the grated Cheddar and onion. With wet hands, shape into 4 rounds, then press down with 2 fingers to form into röstis. Neaten up the edges.

Brush lightly with oil on both sides and grill on a foil-lined grill rack at a medium heat for 2–3 minutes on each side until golden brown.

Serve the röstis warm with the ketchup. (Any that are not needed straight away may be stored in an airtight container in the refrigerator for up to 3 days.)

For potato, bacon & tomato röstis, make the potato mixture as above, omitting the onion. Add 1 finely chopped large tomato and 2 rashers finely chopped cooked streaky bacon to the mixture along with 2 tablespoons tomato ketchup. Shape into 4 patties and cook as above. Use to fill warm toasted wholemeal pitta breads with watercress and extra ketchup.

sweet potato-topped fish pie

Serves **4**
Preparation time **45 minutes**
Cooking time **45 minutes**

375 g (12 oz) **cod fillet**
300 ml (½ pint) **water**
250 g (8 oz) **prawns**, thawed if frozen, drained
1 large **carrot**, roughly chopped
250 g (8 oz) **broccoli**, cut into small florets
25 g (1 oz) **butter**
25 g (1 oz) **plain flour**
300 ml (½ pint) **milk**
50 g (2 oz) **Cheddar cheese**, grated

Potato topping
625 g (1¼ lb) **sweet potatoes**, peeled and chopped
50 g (2 oz) **butter**
3 tablespoons chopped **parsley**
25 g (1 oz) **Cheddar cheese**, finely grated

Place the cod fillet in a medium, heavy-based frying pan and pour over the measured water. Bring to the boil, reduce the heat, cover and simmer for 3 minutes until the fish is opaque and cooked through. Drain and reserve the fish stock. Flake the fish into chunks and gently toss with the prawns.

Cook the carrot and broccoli in boiling water for 5 minutes, drain and set aside. Melt the butter in a pan, remove from the heat and add the flour. Stir over a gentle heat for 30 seconds. Remove from the heat and gradually add the milk a little at a time, stirring well after each addition, then add the reserved fish stock and stir well.

Return the pan to the heat and bring to the boil, stirring continuously until thickened. Remove from the heat and add the Cheddar. Pour over the fish, add the vegetables and very gently fold together. Transfer to a large gratin dish and set aside.

Meanwhile, cook the sweet potatoes for 8–10 minutes until tender. Drain, add the butter and mash well. Stir in the parsley, spoon over the top of the fish and sauce and sprinkle with the Cheddar. Bake in a preheated oven, 200°C (400°F), Gas Mark 6, for 30 minutes until a golden crust forms.

For cheesy tuna & prawn pie, replace the cod with 2 x 200 g (7 oz) cans tuna in brine, drained and flaked. Cook 750 g (1½ lb) white potatoes and mash with the butter, an extra 50 g (2 oz) Cheddar and 6 tablespoons milk. Fold in the parsley, spoon over the pie, sprinkle with the remaining cheese and bake as above.

asian noodles with prawns

Serves **2**
Preparation time **20 minutes**
Cooking time **10 minutes**

3 tablespoons **plum sauce**
2 tablespoons **seasoned rice vinegar**
2 tablespoons **soy sauce**
100 g (3½ oz) fine or medium **egg noodles**
1 tablespoon **vegetable oil**
2 **spring onions**, sliced diagonally into chunky pieces
½ mild **red chilli**, cored, deseeded and finely chopped
150 g (5 oz) **pak choi** or **cabbage**, thinly sliced
100 g (3½ oz) **baby sweetcorn**, cut in half diagonally
200 g (7 oz) peeled **prawns**, thawed if frozen, drained

Mix the plum sauce with the rice vinegar and soy sauce in a small bowl and set aside.

Pour plenty of freshly boiled water into a medium saucepan and bring back to the boil. Add the noodles and cook for 3 minutes. Drain through a colander.

Heat the oil in a large frying pan or wok for 1 minute. Add the spring onions and chilli and fry for 1 minute, stirring with a wooden spoon. Add the pak choi or cabbage and the sweetcorn and fry for a further 2–3 minutes until the vegetables are softened.

Tip the noodles, prawns and sauce into the pan and cook, stirring gently, over a low heat until the ingredients are mixed together and hot. Serve immediately.

For Asian noodles with beef & coconut, replace the red chilli and pak choi with 175 g (6 oz) blanched broccoli florets. Add to the wok with the spring onions and cook for 1 minute. Add 175 g (6 oz) rump steak, cut into thin strips and cook in the pan for a further 2–3 minutes until golden. Add a 400 ml (14 fl oz) can coconut milk with 2 tablespoons soy sauce to replace the plum sauce and toss with the noodles. Heat for 1 minute until hot.

salmon rösti cakes

Serves **6**
Preparation time **30 minutes**
Cooking time **25–30 minutes**

500 g (1 lb) **white potatoes**, peeled but left whole
25 g (1 oz) **butter**
250 g (8 oz) **salmon fillets**
2 tablespoons **sunflower oil**
200 ml (7 fl oz) **crème fraîche**
3 **spring onions**, finely sliced
2 tablespoons chopped **chives**
lemon wedges, to serve

Bring a large pan of lightly salted water to the boil. Cook the potatoes for 10 minutes until beginning to soften. Drain and set aside to cool.

Heat the butter in a small frying pan and add the salmon. Cover with a tight-fitting lid and reduce the heat to very low. Cook for 8–10 minutes until the salmon is just cooked. Remove from the heat and set aside until the salmon is cool enough to handle. Flake the salmon and place in a bowl with the pan juices.

Grate the cooled potatoes, add to the bowl with the salmon and toss together to mix. Divide the mixture into 6 and form into flattened patty shapes. Heat the oil in a large nonstick frying pan and cook the rösti over a moderate heat for 2–3 minutes on each side until golden and cooked through, turning with a fish slice.

Meanwhile, place the crème fraîche in a bowl with the spring onions and chives and mix well. Drain the rösti on kitchen paper, then spoon over the crème fraîche and serve with lemon wedges.

For rösti with bacon & eggs, follow the recipe above, omitting the salmon and adding 1 tablespoon chopped parsley before shaping. Serve the crisp rösti each with 2 lightly fried bacon rashers and a poached egg on top, and homemade ketchup (see pages 26–27).

crumb-topped macaroni cheese

Serves **4**
Preparation time **15 minutes**
Cooking time **about 25 minutes**

200 g (7 oz) **macaroni**
100 g (3½ oz) fresh or frozen **peas**
65 g (2½ oz) **butter**
40 g (1½ oz) **plain flour**
500 ml (17 fl oz) **milk**
1 teaspoon **Dijon mustard**
150 g (5 oz) **Cheddar cheese**, coarsely grated
100 g (3½ oz) **ham**, chopped into small pieces
65 g (2½ oz) **breadcrumbs**

Cook the macaroni for about 10 minutes or according to packet instructions until just tender. Add the peas to the pan and cook for a further 2 minutes. Drain and put on one side.

Melt 40 g (1½ oz) of the butter in the rinsed and dried saucepan. Add the flour and stir it in with a wooden spoon. Cook over a gentle heat, stirring, for 1 minute. Remove the pan from the heat and gradually pour in the milk, whisking well. Return the pan to the heat and cook over a gentle heat, stirring continuously until the sauce is thickened and smooth.

Add the mustard, Cheddar and ham and stir until the cheese has melted. Tip in the macaroni and peas and stir until coated in the sauce, then pour into a shallow heatproof dish.

Melt the remaining butter in a small saucepan and stir in the breadcrumbs until they are coated. Sprinkle the breadcrumbs over the macaroni and cook under a moderate grill for about 5 minutes or until golden, watching closely as the breadcrumbs will brown quickly. Use oven gloves to remove the dish from under the grill, and serve.

For crumb-topped aubergine & macaroni cheese, omit the peas and ham and replace with half a roughly chopped aubergine cooked in 2 tablespoons olive oil until soft, and 3 roughly chopped tomatoes. Top with the crumbs and bake as above.

korma-style curried prawns

Serves **4**
Preparation time **5 minutes**
Cooking time **about 25 minutes**

1 tablespoon **vegetable oil**
1 **onion**, roughly chopped
1 cm (½ inch) piece **root ginger**, peeled and finely grated
1 teaspoon **ground coriander**
½ teaspoon **ground cumin**
½ teaspoon **curry powder**
400 g (13 oz) can **chopped tomatoes**
1 tablespoon **soft brown sugar**
400 ml (13 fl oz) can **coconut milk**
250 g (8 oz) **prawns**, thawed if frozen
125 g (4 oz) frozen **peas**
3 tablespoons chopped **coriander**
rice or **naan**, to serve

Heat the oil in a large nonstick frying pan and cook the onion and ginger over a gentle heat for 3–4 minutes, stirring regularly until soft, but not golden. Add the spices and cook for a further 1 minute. Add the chopped tomatoes and sugar and increase the heat slightly, continuing to cook for a further 5 minutes, stirring occasionally, until the tomatoes have reduced slightly and thickened.

Pour in the coconut milk and bring to the boil. Reduce the heat and simmer, uncovered, for 10 minutes until the sauce has reduced and thickened. Drain the prawns well, then add to the sauce with the peas and coriander and cook for a further 2–3 minutes until piping hot.

Serve the mild curry in warmed serving bowls, with either rice or naan breads to mop up the juices.

For mild chicken & squash curry, omit the ginger and replace the prawns with 250 g (8 oz) roughly chopped chicken breast and the peas with 250 g (8 oz) butternut squash, peeled and cubed. Cook both the chicken and the squash with the onion as above, then add the spices and continue to follow the remaining recipe as above.

lamb hotpot with dumplings

Serves **4**
Preparation time **30 minutes**
Cooking time **about 1 hour**

1 tablespoon **vegetable oil**
1 small **onion**, chopped
375 g (12 oz) boneless **lamb**, cubed
1 **leek**, chopped
75 g (3 oz) ready-to-eat **dried apricots**, chopped
375 g (12 oz) **new potatoes**, halved
1 tablespoon **thyme leaves**
2 tablespoons **plain flour**
600 ml (1 pint) **rich lamb stock**

Dumplings
125 g (4 oz) **plain flour**
½ teaspoon **salt**
1 teaspoon **thyme leaves**
50 g (2 oz) **vegetable suet**
about 4 tablespoons cold **water**

Heat the oil in a large, heavy-based saucepan and cook the onion and lamb over a moderate heat for 4–5 minutes until golden and soft. Add the leek, apricots and new potatoes and cook for 2 minutes, then add the thyme and flour and stir well to coat lightly. Pour in the stock, then bring to the boil and cover and simmer gently for 35 minutes, stirring occasionally.

Meanwhile, make the dumplings. Place the flour and salt in a bowl with the thyme leaves and suet and mix well. Mix in enough water to make an elastic dough. Divide into 12 and shape into small walnut-sized balls using lightly floured hands. Stir the hotpot and top up with a little water if necessary, then drop the dumplings into the stock and cover and simmer for 15 minutes until the dumplings have almost doubled in size.

Serve the hotpot ladled into warm serving bowls with the dumplings.

For vegetable hotpot with cheesy dumplings, omit the lamb and replace with 2 chopped carrots, 1 roughly chopped red pepper and 1 chopped courgette. Also replace the lamb stock with vegetable stock, and cook as above. Add 3 tablespoons raisins with the apricots. Add 25 g (1 oz) finely grated Cheddar cheese to the plain flour when making the dumplings and cook as above.

all-in-one chicken pie

Serves **4**
Preparation time **20 minutes**
Cooking time **45–50 minutes**

250 g (8 oz) **broccoli florets**
1 tablespoon **olive oil**
375 g (12 oz) boneless, skinless **chicken breasts**, cubed
6 **streaky bacon** rashers, chopped
2 small **carrots**, chopped
25 g (1 oz) **butter**
25 g (1 oz) **plain flour**
300 ml (½ pint) **milk**
1 tablespoon **white wine vinegar**
1 teaspoon **Dijon mustard**
200 ml (7 fl oz) **crème fraîche**
2 tablespoons chopped **tarragon** or **parsley**
500 g (1 lb) packet **shortcrust pastry**
beaten **egg**, for glazing

Cook the broccoli for 5 minutes until tender. Drain and refresh with cold water, then set aside. Heat the oil in a nonstick frying pan and cook the chicken and bacon over a moderate heat for 7–8 minutes. Add the carrots and cook for a further 3–4 minutes until golden all over. Remove from the heat.

Heat the butter in a medium saucepan and add the flour. Cook over a gentle heat for a few seconds, then remove from the heat and gradually add the milk until well mixed. Add the vinegar and mustard and mix well. Return to the heat and stir continuously until boiled and thickened. Add the crème fraîche and herbs. Add the chicken and vegetables and stir well to coat, then transfer to a round pie dish.

Roll out the pastry on a floured surface to just larger than the dish. Moisten the rim of the dish lightly with a little water, then place the pastry over the top, trim the edges and decorate with any remaining pastry trimmings if liked. Glaze lightly with the beaten egg. Bake in a preheated oven, 180°C (350°F), Gas Mark 4, for 25–30 minutes until crisp and golden.

For creamy chunky gammon pie, replace the chicken and bacon with a 500 g (1 lb) gammon joint. Half fill a large pan with water, then add 3 peppercorns and a bay leaf. Lower the gammon into the pan, then bring to the boil and cook for 1½ hours. Drain and set aside to cool. Cook the carrots with the broccoli, then cut the gammon into chunks and add the vegetables and gammon to the sauce. Continue as above.

baked cabbage with nuts & cheese

Serves **4**
Preparation time **15 minutes**
Cooking time **30 minutes**

375 g (12 oz) **white cabbage**, shredded
125 g (4 oz) **green** or **savoy cabbage**, shredded
1 teaspoon **ground nutmeg**
125 g (4 oz) roasted unsalted **peanuts**, toasted
25 g (1 oz) **butter**
25 g (1 oz) **plain flour**
450 ml (¾ pint) **milk**
125 g (4 oz) strong **Cheddar cheese**, grated
1 teaspoon **Dijon mustard**
2 tablespoons chopped **parsley**
25 g (1 oz) **wholemeal breadcrumbs**

Cook the two types of cabbage in boiling water for 5 minutes until just tender. Drain and place in a large mixing bowl and toss with the nutmeg and peanuts.

Heat the butter in a nonstick saucepan until melted. Remove from the heat, add the flour and mix to a paste. Return to the heat and cook for a few seconds. Remove from the heat and add the milk a little at a time, stirring well between each addition. Return to the heat and bring to the boil, stirring continuously until boiled and thickened.

Remove the pan from the heat and add 75 g (3 oz) of the grated Cheddar and the mustard. Mix well, then pour over the cabbage and mix it in.

Transfer the mixture to a gratin dish, or 4 individual gratin dishes. Toss the remaining cheese with the parsley and breadcrumbs, then sprinkle over the top and bake in a preheated oven, 200°C (400°F), Gas Mark 6, for 20 minutes until golden and bubbling.

For root vegetable bake with nuts & cheese, replace the cabbage with 375 g (12 oz) sliced butternut squash and 250 g (8 oz) sliced parsnips. Cook in boiling water for 5 minutes and drain. Mix with the nuts and cheese sauce, sprinkle with the cheesy breadcrumbs and bake as above.

supper in a hurry

Serves **4**
Preparation time **25 minutes**
Cooking time **20 minutes**

1 **ciabatta bread loaf**
small handful **chives**
125 g (4 oz) **garlic butter**, softened
5 tablespoons **olive oil**
4 boneless, skinless **chicken breasts**, cut in half horizontally
4 **tomatoes**, sliced
150 g (5 oz) **mozzarella cheese**, drained and sliced
1 tablespoon **white wine vinegar**
1 tablespoon **wholegrain mustard**
1 teaspoon **caster sugar**

Cut the bread at 1.5 cm (¾ inch) intervals, leaving the slices only just attached at the base.

Snip the chives with scissors and mix half in a bowl with the garlic butter. Roughly spread a dot of butter into each cut of the bread. Lay the loaf on a piece of foil and bring the edges up over the top, scrunching them together. Bake in a preheated oven, 220°C (425°F), Gas Mark 7, for 10 minutes.

Meanwhile, heat 1 tablespoon of the oil in a large frying pan. Add the chicken and fry gently for 5 minutes until golden on the underside (check by lifting a piece with a fish slice). Turn the pieces over and fry for a further 5 minutes.

Using oven gloves, carefully open out the foil on the garlic bread and bake for a further 10 minutes.

Scatter the tomato and mozzarella slices in a shallow dish.

Make a dressing by whisking together the remaining oil with the vinegar, mustard and sugar in a bowl. Scatter the remaining chives over the salad and drizzle with the dressing. Using oven gloves, remove the garlic bread from the oven and serve with the salad and chicken.

For speedy breaded pork escalopes, lightly toss 4 pork escalopes in a little flour, dip in 4 beaten eggs and then coat in 200 g (7 oz) wholemeal breadcrumbs tossed with 2 pinches smoked paprika. Heat 3 tablespoons oil in a nonstick frying pan and cook the escalopes for 2–3 minutes on each side until golden. Serve with the tomato and mozzarella salad as above.

butternut squash risotto

Serves **4**
Preparation time **15 minutes**
Cooking time **about 25 minutes**

2 tablespoons **olive oil**
1 **onion**, finely chopped
500 g (1 lb) **butternut squash**, peeled, deseeded and roughly chopped
250 g (8 oz) **arborio rice**
900 ml (1½ pints) **rich chicken stock**
75 g (3 oz) freshly grated **Parmesan cheese**, plus extra to serve
4 tablespoons **pine nuts**, toasted
250 g (8 oz) fresh **spinach leaves**

Heat the oil in a large heavy-based frying pan and cook the onion and squash over a low to moderate heat for 10 minutes until softened. Add the rice and cook for 1 minute, then add half the stock. Bring to the boil, then reduce the heat and simmer gently for 5 minutes until almost all the stock has been absorbed, stirring occasionally.

Continue to add the stock 150 ml (¼ pint) at a time and cook over a gentle heat until the almost all the stock has been absorbed before adding more. Once the rice is tender, remove the pan from the heat, add the Parmesan, pine nuts and spinach and stir well to combine and wilt the spinach, returning to the heat for 1 minute if necessary.

Serve in warmed serving bowls with extra freshly grated Parmesan.

For chicken & pea risotto, replace the butternut squash with 3 x 150 g (5 oz) chicken breasts, chopped and cooked with the onion. Cook in the same way as above, adding an additional 125 g (4 oz) frozen peas and adding the spinach if liked. Serve with extra Parmesan sprinkled over.

on-the-run suppers

tasty teatime pasties

Makes **6**
Preparation time **25 minutes**, plus chilling
Cooking time **25 minutes**

375 g (12 oz) **plain flour**
½ teaspoon **salt**
175 g (6 oz) **butter**, cubed
2–3 tablespoons cold **water**
1 tablespoon **vegetable oil**
½ small **onion**, chopped
175 g (6 oz) lean **lamb**, finely sliced
1 small **potato** or 2 **baby new potatoes**, peeled and diced
300 ml (½ pint) hot **lamb stock**
1 teaspoon **Dijon mustard**, optional
2 tablespoons finely chopped **mint**
beaten **egg**

Sift the flour and salt into a large mixing bowl and add the butter. Rub the butter into the flour until the mixture resembles fine breadcrumbs. Add the measured water and mix to form a rough dough. Turn on to a lightly floured work surface and knead until smooth. Place in a food bag and refrigerate for 30 minutes.

Meanwhile, heat the oil in a frying pan and cook the onion and lamb over a moderate heat for 5 minutes, stirring occasionally, until beginning to brown. Add the potato, reduce the heat and cook for a further 2 minutes, stirring occasionally until beginning to brown.

Mix the lamb stock with the mustard and pour into the pan. Cover with a tight-fitting lid and simmer gently for 15 minutes, stirring occasionally until the potatoes are soft yet still retaining their shape, and the meat is tender. Stir in the mint and set aside to cool.

Roll out the pastry to 5 mm (¼ inch) thick, and using a 15 cm (6 inch) saucer as a template, cut out 6 rounds. Lightly brush the edges of each of the circles with a little water and place 2 tablespoons of the mixture in the centre of each. Fold up to enclose the filling and pinch and gently twist the edges to seal. Place on a baking sheet and lightly glaze each one with the beaten egg. Bake in a preheated oven, 200°C (400°F), Gas Mark 6, for 20–25 minutes until the pastry is golden and crisp. Wrap loosely in foil to keep warm.

spanish tortilla

Serves **8**
Preparation time **10 minutes**
Cooking time **20–25 minutes**

2 tablespoons **olive oil**
2 **onions**, sliced
1 **garlic clove**, crushed
500 g (1 lb) cooked **waxy potatoes**, sliced
6 **eggs**
50 ml (2 fl oz) **milk**

Heat 1 tablespoon of the olive oil in a medium frying pan, with a metal handle, over a low heat and add the onions and garlic. Cook for 5 minutes until golden, then add the cooked potatoes and heat through.

Meanwhile, in a large bowl, beat together the eggs and milk. Add the potatoes, onion and garlic to the egg mixture and stir well.

Return the pan to the heat, and heat the remaining oil. Tip the potato and egg mixture into the pan and cook over a low heat for 7–8 minutes, until beginning to set. Preheat the grill to a medium heat and cook the tortilla in its pan under the grill for 3–5 minutes until the top is golden and set.

Turn out the tortilla on to a plate and allow to cool. Cut into slices and serve warm or cold. (You can wrap any unused tortilla securely and refrigerate it – eat within 3 days.)

For meaty chorizo Spanish tortilla, layer the potatoes with a 75 g (3 oz) packet sliced chorizo and 2 tablespoons chopped parsley and cook as above. Serve either warm or cold with cherry tomatoes.

mini quiches

Makes **18**
Preparation time **45 minutes**
Cooking time **20 minutes**

vegetable oil, for greasing
plain flour, for dusting
375 g (12 oz) ready-rolled **shortcrust pastry**, thawed if frozen and taken out of the refrigerator 15 minutes before use
2 **eggs**
200 ml (7 fl oz) **milk**
4 slices **ham**, diced
2 **spring onions**, chopped
5 **cherry tomatoes**, chopped
50 g (2 oz) **Cheddar cheese**, grated

Smear some oil all around the cups of 2 bun tins. Sprinkle some flour on to a work surface and unroll the pastry. Flatten it with the balls of your hands. Stamp circles out of the pastry with a cutter and place each circle in a cup of the tin, gently pressing it down with your fingertips.

Place the eggs and milk in a measuring jug and beat with a fork.

Put the ham, spring onions and cherry tomatoes in a bowl and mix together. Put a dessertspoonful of the mixture into each pastry cup.

Pour some of the egg and milk mixture into each cup. Sprinkle some Cheddar over the top. Bake the quiches in a preheated oven, 220°C (425°F), Gas Mark 7, for 20 minutes or until set and golden. Serve the quiches hot or cold.

For red pepper, garlic & Parmesan quiches, replace the ham, spring onions and cherry tomatoes with the following – heat 1 tablespoon olive oil in a small pan and cook 1 roughly chopped red pepper and 1 crushed garlic clove for 2–3 minutes until soft. Place in the pastry cases with 50 g (2 oz) freshly grated Parmesan cheese and pour over the egg and milk as above. Omit the Cheddar and bake as above.

no-mess cheesy pepperoni calzones

Serves **8**
Preparation time **30–40 minutes**
Cooking time **25–30 minutes**

300 g (10 oz) **pizza dough mix**
flour, for dusting
1 tablespoon **olive oil**
1 small **red pepper**, cored, deseeded and roughly chopped
1 small **yellow pepper**, cored, deseeded and roughly chopped
175 g (6 oz) **chorizo sausage**, sliced
1 large **tomato**, roughly chopped
½ teaspoon mixed **dried herbs**
150 g (5 oz) packet **mozzarella cheese**, drained and cubed

Make up the pizza dough according to packet instructions and turn out on to a lightly floured surface. Divide the dough into 8 pieces. Knead each lightly to produce smooth rounds, then roll into a 20 cm (8 inch) circle. Loosely cover with clingfilm.

Heat the oil in a large, nonstick frying pan and cook the peppers over a moderate heat for 5 minutes, stirring occasionally. Add the chorizo slices and cook for 2 minutes before adding the tomato. Cook for a further 3–4 minutes, stirring occasionally, until the tomato has softened. Remove from the heat and stir in the herbs and mozzarella.

Allow to cool slightly before dividing the filling between the 8 dough circles. Lightly brush the edges with a little water, then fold the circles in half to enclose the filling and press to seal. Place on a baking sheet and bake in a preheated oven, 220°C (425°F), Gas Mark 7, for 15–20 minutes. Serve warm.

For butternut squash & feta cheese calzones, heat 1 tablespoon olive oil in a pan and cook 250 g (8 oz) cubed butternut squash over a moderate heat for 5–6 minutes until beginning to soften. Add 5 tablespoons water, cover and cook over a gentle heat for 3 minutes. Remove from the heat and allow to cool. Add 2 tablespoons chopped parsley and 100 g (4 oz) crumbled feta. Use the filling as above.

mini scone pizzas

Serves **4**
Preparation time **25 minutes**
Cooking time **15–20 minutes**

250 g (8 oz) **self-raising wholemeal flour**
50 g (2 oz) **butter**, cubed
150 ml (¼ pint) **milk**
150 ml (¼ pint) **tomato passata**
3 tablespoons **tomato purée**
2 tablespoons chopped **basil**
4 thick slices good-quality **ham**, shredded
125 g (4 oz) **pitted black olives**, halved
150 g (5 oz) **mozzarella cheese**, grated

Sift the flour into a bowl and rub in the butter until the mixture resembles fine breadcrumbs. Make a well in the centre and stir in enough of the milk to give a fairly soft dough. Turn it out on to a lightly floured surface and knead gently. Cut into 4 pieces, then knead again to shape each into a rough round. Roll out 4 rough circles each to about 15 cm (6 inch) and place on a baking sheet.

Mix together the passata, tomato purée and basil. Divide between the scone bases and spread to within 1 cm (½ inch) of the edges. Pile each with the ham and olives, then sprinkle with the mozzarella.

Drizzle with a little oil and bake in a preheated oven, 200°C (400°F), Gas Mark 6, for 15–20 minutes until the bases are risen and the cheese is golden. Wrap in foil and serve warm or cold.

For egg & bacon scone pizzas, form each pizza base into a slight bowl shape with a ridge around the edge. Spread with the tomato sauce. Heat 1 tablespoon olive oil and cook 6 roughly chopped back bacon rashers for 2 minutes until golden. Drain on kitchen paper. Sprinkle the pizzas with the bacon pieces, then crack an egg over the top of each. Bake in the oven as above without the cheese. Remove from the oven and, while still warm, sprinkle each with 1 tablespoon grated mozzarella and some chopped parsley.

vegetable burgers

Serves **8**
Preparation time **20 minutes**, plus chilling
Cooking time **12–15 minutes**

250 g (8 oz) **spinach**, washed and patted dry
1 tablespoon **olive oil**
1 small **red pepper**, cored, deseeded and very finely chopped
4 **spring onions**, finely sliced
400 g (13 oz) can **chickpeas**, drained and rinsed
125 g (4 oz) **ricotta cheese**
1 **egg yolk**
½ teaspoon **ground coriander**
50 g (2 oz) **plain flour**
1 **egg**, beaten
175 g (6 oz) **wholemeal breadcrumbs**
4 tablespoons **vegetable oil**

To serve
8 mini **burger buns**
tomato ketchup (optional, see pages 26–27)
cherry tomatoes (optional)

Put the moist spinach in a pan over a moderate heat for 2–3 minutes, stirring continuously, until wilted. Remove from the heat, drain well, and set aside.

Heat the olive oil in a frying pan and cook the pepper and spring onions over a moderate heat for 4–5 minutes until soft. Set aside.

Place the chickpeas in a food processor with the ricotta and blend until smooth. Add the spinach, egg yolk and coriander and blend again to mix well. Transfer to a mixing bowl and fold in the pepper and spring onion mixture. Shape the mixture into 8 patties, toss them lightly in the flour, then roll first in the beaten egg and then in the breadcrumbs, to coat. Chill for 30 minutes.

Heat the vegetable oil in a large, heavy-based frying pan and cook the burgers over a moderate heat for 6–7 minutes, turning once, until golden and crisp. Serve in the buns with tomato ketchup and cherry tomatoes, if liked.

For sausage & pepper burgers, cook the spinach, peppers and onions as above. Chop the spinach roughly. Place 375 g (12 oz) good-quality sausagemeat in a bowl and add 1 tablespoon tomato chutney and 1 teaspoon Dijon mustard. Mix well, then stir in the spinach, peppers and onions and mix well. Do not coat, but simply heat the oil and cook for 2–3 minutes on each side until golden. Serve as above.

multicoloured root chips

Serves **4**
Preparation time **15 minutes**
Cooking time **25–30 minutes**

2 **sweet potatoes**, cut into slim wedges with skin on
1 large **baking potato**, cut into slim wedges with skin on
2 **parsnips**, cut into long wedges
3 tablespoons **olive oil**
1 teaspoon **Cajun seasoning**
3 tablespoons chopped **parsley**

Mayonnaise
1 **egg**
150 ml (¼ pint) **olive oil**
½ teaspoon **mustard powder**
1 tablespoon **white wine vinegar**
1 tablespoon chopped **parsley**

Put the sweet potato, baking potato and parsnip wedges in a bowl and drizzle with the olive oil, tossing well to coat lightly. Sprinkle with the Cajun seasoning and toss again to coat. Transfer to a large baking sheet and roast in a preheated oven, 200°C (400°F), Gas Mark 6, for 25–30 minutes, until the vegetables are crisp and golden.

Meanwhile, make the mayonnaise. Place all the ingredients except the parsley in a small measuring jug, and using an electric blender whiz until a thick mayonnaise is formed. Stir in the parsley.

Serve the chips tossed with the parsley, with a tub of the mayonnaise, to dip.

For cheese & chive mayonnaise to serve as an alternative accompaniment, make the mayonnaise as above and stir in 2 tablespoons soured cream, 1 tablespoon freshly grated Parmesan cheese and 2 tablespoons fresh snipped chives. Serve with the root chips, to dip.

crispy lamb moroccan rolls

Serves **2**
Preparation time **15 minutes**
Cooking time **10 minutes**

250 g (8 oz) **lamb mince**
1 teaspoon **ground cinnamon**
3 tablespoons **pine nuts**
2 **naan breads**, warmed
200 g (7 oz) **hummus**
2 tablespoons **mint leaves**
1 **Little Gem lettuce**, finely shredded (optional)

Fry the mince in a large, nonstick frying pan for 8–10 minutes until it becomes golden brown. Add the cinnamon and pine nuts and cook again for 1 minute. Remove from the heat.

Place the warm naan breads on a chopping board and, using a rolling pin, firmly roll to flatten.

Mix the hummus with half the mint leaves, then spread in a thick layer over the warmed naans. Spoon over the crispy lamb, then scatter over the shredded lettuce, if using, and the remaining mint leaves. Tightly roll up and secure with cocktail sticks. Serve immediately, or wrap tightly in foil to transport.

For lamb kofta, mix the raw mince with 4 finely chopped spring onions, 1 teaspoon ground cinnamon, a very finely chopped tomato and 1 egg yolk until blended together. Form into a very large, thin patty shape, and grill or cook in a large, heavy-based frying pan on one side for 3 minutes, then on the other side for 2 minutes, until golden. Spread 1 warm naan with 2 tablespoons Greek yogurt, scatter with the mint leaves and shredded lettuce, if using and slip the large flattened kofta on top. Roll tightly and secure with cocktail sticks. Cut the kofta in half to serve 2.

chickpea & herb salad

Serves **4**
Preparation time **10 minutes**
Cooking time **5 minutes** (optional)

100 g (3½ oz) **bulgar wheat**
4 tablespoons **olive oil**
1 tablespoon **lemon juice**
2 tablespoons chopped **flat leaf parsley**
1 tablespoon chopped **mint**
400 g (13 oz) can **chickpeas**, drained and rinsed
125 g (4 oz) **cherry tomatoes**, halved
1 tablespoon chopped mild **onion**
100 g (3½ oz) **cucumber**, diced
150 g (5 oz) **feta cheese**, diced

Put the bulgar wheat in a heatproof bowl and pour over sufficient boiling water just to cover. Set aside until the water has been absorbed. (If you want to give a fluffier finish to the bulgar wheat, transfer it to a steamer and steam for 5 minutes. Spread out on a plate to cool.)

Mix together the oil, lemon juice, parsley and mint in a large bowl. Add the chickpeas, tomatoes, onion, cucumber and bulgar wheat. Mix well and add the feta, stirring lightly to avoid breaking up the cheese.

Serve immediately, or pack into an airtight container to transport.

For tuna, bean & black olive salad, replace the chickpeas, tomatoes, onion and cucumber for 1 x 200 g (7 oz) can tuna, drained and flaked, 1 x 400 g (13 oz) can mixed beans, drained and rinsed, 100 g (4 oz) black olives and 4 tablespoons lemon juice. Toss well before serving.

sweetcorn fritters & tomato dip

Makes **20**
Preparation time **15 minutes**
Cooking time **20–30 minutes**

75 g (3 oz) **plain flour**
½ teaspoon **paprika**
150 ml (¼ pint) **milk**
1 **egg**, beaten
275 g (9 oz) can **sweetcorn**, drained
3 tablespoons chopped **parsley**
2 **spring onions**, finely chopped
½ **red pepper**, finely chopped

Tomato dip
1 tablespoon **olive oil**
6 ripe **tomatoes**, roughly chopped
1 tablespoon **soft brown sugar**
½ teaspoon **paprika**
1 tablespoon **red wine vinegar**
4 tablespoons **vegetable oil**

Sift the flour and paprika into a bowl, then add the milk and egg and whisk together to form a thick batter. Add the sweetcorn, parsley, spring onions and red pepper and mix well. If the mixture is too thick, add 1 tablespoon water to loosen. Set aside while making the tomato dip.

Heat the oil in a medium heavy-based pan, add the tomatoes and cook over a moderate heat for 5 minutes, stirring occasionally. Add the sugar, paprika and vinegar, reduce the heat, cover and simmer over a very gentle heat for 10–15 minutes, stirring occasionally until the tomatoes are thick and pulpy. Remove from the heat and transfer to a bowl to cool.

Heat the vegetable oil in a large, nonstick frying pan and spoon tablespoons of the sweetcorn mixture into the pan, well spaced apart, and cook for 1–2 minutes on each side, in batches, until golden and firm. Remove the fritters from the pan using a fish slice and drain on kitchen paper.

Serve the sweetcorn fritters with a pot of the sauce, to dip or wrap in foil to keep warm for transport.

For minted courgette fritters, replace the sweetcorn with 1 finely chopped large courgette. Heat 1 teaspoon of oil in a large frying pan and cook the courgette over a moderate heat for 3–4 minutes, stirring occasionally until pale golden. Add to the batter with 2 tablespoons of chopped mint.

chicken & bacon wraps

Serves **2**
Preparation time **15 minutes**
Cooking time **5 minutes**

1 tablespoon **olive oil**
2 x 150 g (5 oz) boneless, skinless **chicken breasts**
2 **unsmoked back bacon** rashers
2 **soft flour tortillas**
4 tablespoons **mayonnaise**
2 handfuls **spinach**

Lightly oil 2 sheets of clingfilm with the oil. Place the 2 chicken breasts, well spaced apart, between the 2 clingfilm sheets and bash with a rolling pin until the chicken is 5 mm (¼ inch) thick.

Heat a griddle or heavy-based frying pan and cook the chicken for 5 minutes, turning once, until golden and cooked through, adding the bacon to the pan for the final 2 minutes.

Spread the tortillas each with 2 tablespoons mayonnaise. Place the chicken breast over the top, then lay 2 bacon rashers on top of the chicken. Sprinkle with the spinach, then roll up tightly, securing with cocktail sticks. Cut in half and serve immediately, or wrap tightly in greaseproof paper and secure with string to transport.

For tuna & coleslaw wraps, drain a 200 g (7 oz) can of tuna in brine, and mix with 2 roughly chopped tomatoes and 1 tablespoon chopped chives. Mix ⅛ cabbage, finely shredded, with 1 large grated carrot and 1 teaspoon poppy seeds and set aside. Mix 4 tablespoons mayonnaise with 2 tablespoons water until well blended, then pour over the cabbage and carrot and toss to mix. Spread the tuna mixture over 4 flour tortillas, then spoon over the coleslaw. Roll tightly and secure with cocktail sticks as above.

green bean & bacon frittata

Serves **4**
Preparation time **10 minutes**
Cooking time **about 10 minutes**

175 g (6 oz) **fine green beans**
6 **back bacon** rashers
100 g (4 oz) frozen **peas**, defrosted
6 **eggs**
1 teaspoon **wholegrain mustard**
½ teaspoon **ground paprika**
2 tablespoons **vegetable oil**
4 tablespoons freshly grated **Parmesan cheese**

Cook the green beans in boiling water for 5 minutes. Drain and refresh with cold water to stop them from cooking further, then roughly chop and set aside. Meanwhile, place the bacon under a preheated medium grill for 3–4 minutes until golden and cooked. Cool slightly, then snip roughly with scissors. Toss the green beans and bacon with the peas.

Beat the eggs with the mustard and paprika. Heat the oil in a medium nonstick frying pan with a metal handle, then pour in the eggs. Working quickly, scatter over the beans, peas and bacon. Cook over a gentle heat until the base has set.

Sprinkle over the Parmesan and place the pan under the grill for 2–3 minutes until the frittata is set and golden.

Cut the frittata into wedges. If not serving immediately, wrap it in foil to keep warm.

For mushroom & bacon frittata, omit the beans and peas. Heat 1 tablespoon olive oil in a frying pan and cook 250 g (8 oz) quartered chestnut mushrooms for 4–5 minutes until soft and golden. Pour into the egg mixture in the pan and cook as above, with the Parmesan sprinkled over before grilling. Serve cut into wedges, either warm or cold.

café alternatives

lightly spiced chicken nuggets

Serves **4**
Preparation time **15 minutes**
Cooking time **15–20 minutes**

50 g (2 oz) **plain flour**
4 x 150 g (5 oz) boneless, skinless **chicken breasts**, cut into bite-sized chunks
1 **egg**, beaten
150 g (5 oz) **fine wholemeal breadcrumbs**
1 teaspoon **Cajun spice**
2 tablespoons chopped **parsley**
Tomato Ketchup (see pages 26–27), to dip

Place the flour on a plate and toss the chicken in it.

Pour the beaten egg on to a plate. Mix the breadcrumbs with the Cajun spice and parsley on a separate plate. Dip each of the chicken pieces in the beaten egg, then toss in the seasoned breadcrumbs and place on a large baking sheet.

Bake the chicken nuggets in a preheated oven, 200°C (400°F), Gas Mark 6, for 15–20 minutes until golden and cooked through.

Serve hot with tomato ketchup to dip, if liked.

For salmon goujons, replace the chicken with salmon fillets. Cut the fillets into chunks or strips and toss in breadcrumbs seasoned with the finely grated zest of 1 lemon, instead of Cajun spice, and the parsley as above. Bake for 10–15 minutes and serve with mayonnaise flavoured with the juice from the lemon.

ham & fresh pineapple pizza

Serves **4**
Preparation time **25 minutes**, plus rising
Cooking time **about 20 minutes**

250 g (8 oz) **wholemeal plain flour**
½ teaspoon **salt**
1 teaspoon fast-action **dried yeast**
150 ml (¼ pint) warm **water**
1 tablespoon **olive oil**, plus extra for oiling

Topping
2 tablespoons **olive oil**
1 small **onion**, finely chopped
150 ml (¼ pint) **passata**
3 tablespoons **tomato purée**
3 slices good-quality, thick **ham**, cut into strips
2 thick rings of fresh **pineapple**, cut into chunks
150 g (5 oz) **mozzarella cheese**, thinly sliced
thyme leaves, to garnish (optional)

Sift the flour and salt into a bowl, add the yeast and mix well. Make a well in the centre and add the measured water and oil. Stir until it forms a wet dough, then beat for 2 minutes. Turn the dough out on to a well floured surface and knead for about 2 minutes until it becomes smooth and elastic. Roll out to a 30 cm (12 inch) circle, and place on a lightly oiled baking sheet. Cover with lightly oiled clingfilm and leave in a warm place while making the topping.

Heat 1 tablespoon of the oil in a small frying pan and cook the onion over a moderate heat for 2–3 minutes. Remove from the heat and add the passata and tomato purée. Spread over the pizza base to within 2.5 cm (1 inch) of the edges, and scatter over the ham.

Toss the pineapple with the remaining oil. Scatter it over the ham, then top with the mozzarella. Bake in a preheated oven, 220°C (425°F), Gas Mark 7, for 15–18 minutes until golden. Scatter with thyme leaves, if liked.

For chicken & chorizo pizza, replace the ham and pineapple with 2 x 150 g (5 oz) boneless, skinless chicken breasts and 100 g (4 oz) chorizo sausage, both thinly sliced. Heat 1 tablespoon olive oil in a frying pan and cook the chicken over a moderate heat for 3–4 minutes until golden. Add the chorizo and fry for a further 1 minute. Toss with 3 tablespoons fresh basil and pile on to the pizza base, then top with the mozzarella. Omit the thyme.

chicken satay skewers

Serves **4**
Preparation time **20 minutes**, plus marinating
Cooking time **8–10 minutes**

6 tablespoons **dark soy sauce**
2 tablespoons **sesame oil**
1 teaspoon **Chinese 5-spice powder**
375 g (12 oz) boneless, skinless **chicken breasts**, cut into long, thin strips

Sauce
4 tablespoons **peanut butter**
1 tablespoon **dark soy sauce**
½ teaspoon **ground coriander**
½ teaspoon **ground cumin**
pinch of **paprika** or **chilli powder**
8 tablespoons **water**
cucumber, cut into strips, to serve

Place the soy sauce, sesame oil and 5-spice powder into a bowl and mix. Add the chicken and toss together to coat in the marinade. Cover and set aside for 1 hour, stirring occasionally.

Thread the chicken, zigzag fashion, on to 10 soaked bamboo skewers (soaking them in warm water for 30 minutes will prevent the sticks burning while cooking), and place the chicken under a hot grill for 8–10 minutes, turning once, until golden and cooked through.

Meanwhile, put all the sauce ingredients in a small pan and heat, stirring, until warm and well mixed. Transfer to a small serving bowl.

Place the bowl of sauce on a serving plate with the cucumber on one side and the hot chicken skewers around it.

For pork satay skewers, replace the chicken with 375 g (12 oz) pork fillet, cut into long strips along its length. Complete and cook as above. For children who can handle a hotter sauce, fry ½ small red chilli, finely chopped, in 1 teaspoon cooking oil and add to the peanut sauce.

mini steak burgers

Makes **8**
Preparation time **10 minutes**, plus chilling
Cooking time **12–15 minutes**

375 g (12 oz) **fine steak mince**
2 tablespoons **tomato ketchup**
1 tablespoon **wholegrain mustard**
3 tablespoons chopped **chives**
1 tablespoon **olive oil**
100 g (4 oz) **chestnut mushrooms**, sliced
8 thin slices **Gruyère cheese**

To serve
4 **mini burger buns**, cut in half
ketchup or **sauces**

Place the mince in a bowl with the ketchup, mustard and chives. Mix really well together, working the mixture with a fork to grind and blend the ingredients. Shape into 8 patties and place on a plate. Cover with clingfilm and chill for 30 minutes to firm.

Heat the oil in a large frying or griddle pan and cook the mushrooms over a high heat for 3–4 minutes until golden and soft. Remove from the pan using a slotted spoon. Add the burgers and cook over a moderate heat for 4–5 minutes on each side until golden and cooked through. Sit a Gruyère slice on top of each of the burgers and cover with a baking sheet for 1 minute to allow the cheese to soften.

Top the base of each bun with a burger, then spoon over the mushrooms and spread the top half of each bun with ketchup or a sauce of the child's choice. Place the lids on, and serve.

For pork & apple burgers, replace the steak mince with 375 g (12 oz) good-quality pork mince. Core 1 eating apple and grate with the skin on. Add to the mince with the mustard and chives and blend well together using a fork. Form into 8 patties, and cook as above.

sweet & sour pork noodles

Serves **4**
Preparation time **15 minutes**
Cooking time **12–16 minutes**

8 tablespoons **tomato ketchup**
3 tablespoons **soft brown sugar**
2 tablespoons **white wine vinegar**
175 g (6 oz) medium **egg noodles**
2 tablespoons **sesame oil**
375 g (12 oz) lean **pork**, cut into strips
2.5 cm (1 inch) piece fresh **root ginger**, peeled and chopped
1 **garlic clove**, crushed
125 g (4 oz) **mangetouts**, halved in length
1 large **carrot**, cut into strips
175 g (6 oz) **bean sprouts**
200 g (7 oz) can **bamboo shoots**, drained

Place the ketchup, sugar and vinegar in a small saucepan and heat gently for 2–3 minutes until the sugar has dissolved, then set aside.

Cook the egg noodles for 3–5 minutes or according to packet instructions until tender, then drain and set aside.

Heat the oil in a wok or large, heavy-based frying pan and cook the pork strips over a high heat for 2–3 minutes until beginning to turn golden, then add the ginger, garlic, mangetouts and carrot. Stir-fry for a further 2 minutes, then add the bean sprouts and bamboo shoots and stir-fry for 1 minute until all the ingredients are piping hot.

Add the warm, drained noodles and sauce and toss over the heat, using 2 spoons to mix really well and heat through. Serve in warmed serving bowls.

For prawn stir-fry with a thickened soy sauce, heat the oil and cook the ginger, garlic, mangetouts and carrot for 2–3 minutes, then add the bean sprouts and bamboo shoots and 250 g (8 oz) prawns and stir-fry for 1–2 minutes. Replace the sauce ingredients with 150 ml (¼ pint) soy sauce, gently heated in a small pan. Add 1 tablespoon cornflour blended with 2 tablespoons water and ½ teaspoon Chinese 5-spice powder. Stir until warmed and thickened, then remove from the heat. Add to the stir-fry, toss and serve.

prawn toasts

Serves **4**
Preparation time **15 minutes**
Cooking time **about 5 minutes**

175 g (6 oz) **prawns**
2.5 cm (1 inch) piece fresh **root ginger**, peeled and finely grated
1 **spring onion**, finely chopped
1 **egg white**, beaten
1 tablespoon **cornflour**
1 teaspoon **sesame oil**
1 teaspoon **dark soy sauce**, plus extra to serve
4 medium-cut slices **'best of both' bread**
4 tablespoons **sesame seeds**
6 tablespoons **vegetable oil**

Place the prawns in a food processor with the ginger, spring onion, egg white, cornflour, sesame oil and soy sauce and whiz to form a thick paste.

Spread the mixture on each of the slices of bread. Place the sesame seeds on a large plate and press the prawn toast, prawn side down, in the seeds to lightly cover.

Heat 2 tablespoons of the oil in a large, heavy-based frying pan. Cook 2 of the prawn toasts, prawn side down first for 1–2 minutes until golden; then turn over and cook the other side for 1 minute until golden. Repeat the process wiping out the pan with kitchen paper and heating the remaining oil first. Drain on kitchen paper, then cut into triangles.

Serve the toasts with plenty of cucumber and sweetcorn salsa (see below), if liked.

For cucumber & sweetcorn salsa to serve as an accompaniment, finely chop ¼ cucumber and place in a bowl with 4 tablespoons chopped fresh coriander and a 200 g (7 oz) can sweetcorn, drained. Finely chop ½ red pepper and add to the mix, then add 1 tablespoon sweet chilli sauce and mix together. Spoon on to the sesame prawn toasts to serve.

fish & chips in paper cones

Serves **4**
Preparation time **20 minutes**
Cooking time **30–40 minutes**

750 g (1½ lb) **baking potatoes**, cut into thick chips
2 tablespoons **olive oil**
125 g (4 oz) **wholemeal breadcrumbs**
finely grated rind of 1 **lemon**
3 tablespoons chopped **parsley**
4 x 150 g (5 oz) chunky **white fish fillets**, each cut into 4 chunky pieces or goujons
50 g (2 oz) **plain flour**
1 **egg**, beaten
Tomato Ketchup (see pages 26–27), to serve

Toss the potato chips with the oil, then roast in a preheated oven, 200°C (400°F), Gas Mark 6, for 30–40 minutes, turning occasionally until golden and crisp.

Meanwhile, toss the breadcrumbs with the lemon rind and parsley on a plate. Lightly coat the fish goujons in the flour, then the beaten egg, and finally the breadcrumbs. Place on a baking sheet and roast in a preheated oven, 200°C (400°F), Gas Mark 6, for the final 20 minutes of the chips' cooking time, until the fish is opaque and cooked through.

Roll 4 sheets of A5 paper into cones and seal with tape. Place in a bottle holder to help load each with chips, and place 4 goujons on top. Allow the kids to eat these healthy fish and chips with their fingers, dipping them into the ketchup for good measure!

For lemony mayonnaise dip to serve as an alternative accompaniment, place 1 egg, 150 ml (¼ pint) olive oil and 1 tablespoon white wine vinegar in a jug and whiz with a hand blender until a thick mayonnaise is formed. Fold in the grated rind of 1 small lemon and 2 tablespoons of the juice, along with 2 tablespoons chopped parsley.

chicken fajitas & no-chilli salsa

Serves **4**
Preparation time **20 minutes**
Cooking time **about 5 minutes**

½ teaspoon **ground coriander**
½ teaspoon **ground cumin**
½ teaspoon **ground paprika**
1 **garlic clove**, crushed
3 tablespoons chopped **fresh coriander**
375 g (12 oz) boneless, skinless **chicken breasts**, cut into bite-sized strips
1 tablespoon **olive oil**
4 **soft flour tortillas**
soured cream, to serve (optional)

Salsa
3 large, ripe **tomatoes**, finely chopped
3 tablespoons chopped **fresh coriander**
⅛ **cucumber**, finely chopped
1 tablespoon **olive oil**

Guacamole
1 large **avocado**, roughly chopped
grated rind and juice of ½ **lime**
2 teaspoons **sweet chilli sauce** (optional)

Place all the ground spices, garlic and coriander in a mixing bowl. Toss the chicken in the oil, then add to the spices and toss to coat lightly in the spice mixture.

Make the salsa, mix the tomatoes, coriander and cucumber in a bowl and drizzle over the oil. Transfer to a serving bowl.

Make the guacamole, mash the avocado with the lime rind and juice and sweet chilli sauce, if using, until soft and rough-textured. Transfer to a serving bowl.

Heat a griddle pan or heavy-based frying pan and cook the chicken for 3–4 minutes, turning occasionally, until golden and cooked through. Fill the tortillas with the hot chicken slices, guacamole and salsa, and fold into quarters. Spoon over a little soured cream, if liked.

For beef fajitas, replace the chicken with rump or sirloin steak, cut into bite-sized strips. For a slightly 'warmer' version, replace the paprika with mild chilli powder.

cheese & bacon pastries

Serves **6**
Preparation time **15 minutes**
Cooking time **20–25 minutes**

500 g (1 lb oz) packet **puff pastry**
flour, for dusting
2 teaspoon **Dijon mustard** (optional)
50 g (2 oz) **Gruyère cheese**, thinly sliced
50 g (2 oz) **Cheddar cheese**, thinly sliced
3 tablespoons chopped **parsley**
6 **back bacon** rashers, thinly sliced
beaten **egg**

Roll out the pastry on a lightly floured surface to a rectangle measuring 30 x 45 cm (12 x 18 inches). Cut the pastry into 6 x 15 cm (6 inch) squares.

Spread the pastry all over with a thin layer of mustard. Arrange the Gruyère and Cheddar slices on each of the pastry squares in a diagonal line. Sprinkle with the parsley, then ruffle the bacon across the top. Lightly brush the pastry edges with a little warm water, then fold each of the opposite corners up and over the filling to meet, then press to seal with a fork. Place on a baking sheet.

Lightly brush the pastries with beaten egg and bake in a preheated oven, 200°C (400°F), Gas Mark 6, for 20–25 minutes until golden. Serve warm.

For haloumi & tomato pastries, replace the bacon and cheeses with 175 g (6 oz) haloumi cheese, thinly sliced, and 125 g (4 oz) halved cherry tomatoes. Arrange on top of the mustard-spread pastry and sprinkle with the parsley. Bake as above until golden.

super snacks

banana & raisin flapjacks

Makes **12**
Preparation time **10 minutes**
Cooking time **10 minutes**

150 g (5 oz) **butter**
150 ml (¼ pint) **maple syrup**
125 g (4 oz) **raisins**
2 large **bananas**, well mashed
375 g (12 oz) **porridge oats**

Place the butter in a medium pan with the maple syrup and melt over a gentle heat. Stir in the raisins. Remove from the heat and add the bananas, stirring well. Add the oats and stir well until all the oats have been coated.

Spoon the mixture into a 28 x 18 cm (11 x 7 inch) nonstick Swiss roll tin and level the surface using a potato masher for ease. Bake in a preheated oven, 190°C (375°F), Gas Mark 5, for 10 minutes until the top is just beginning to turn a pale golden. The mixture will still seem somewhat soft.

Allow to cool for 10 minutes in the tin before cutting into 12 squares. Remove from the tin and allow to cool completely.

For ginger flapjacks, add 1 teaspoon ground ginger to the melted butter and maple syrup and replace the bananas with 75 g (3 oz) finely chopped stem ginger. Stir through with the raisins and spoon into the prepared tin and level. Bake and cut into squares as above.

bread monsters

Makes **8**
Preparation time **30 minutes**, plus rising
Cooking time **15–20 minutes**

350 g (11½ oz) **strong white flour**, plus extra for dusting
1 teaspoon **salt**
3 g (⅛ oz) fast-action **dried yeast**
1 tablespoon **vegetable oil**
200 ml (7 fl oz) **warm water**
12 **currants**, cut in half, for the eyes and mouths
1 **egg**, beaten

Sift the flour and salt together in a mixing bowl and add the yeast, oil and water. Mix everything together with a wooden spoon, then use your hands to draw the mixture together into a firm dough. If the mixture is too dry to come together, add a little more water. If the mixture sticks to your hands, add some more flour.

Turn the dough out on to a well-floured surface and knead thoroughly for at least 5 minutes, then divide it into 8 equal pieces and knead into balls. Make a pointy snout at one end of each ball and place on a baking sheet lined with nonstick baking paper. Leave plenty of space between the rolls as they will double in size. Make prickles on the monsters by snipping into the dough with the tips of scissors. Press the currant halves into the dough to make the eyes and mouths.

Cover the rolls with a clean tea towel, then leave in a warm place for 1 hour or until they have doubled in size.

Brush the rolls with the beaten egg and bake in a preheated oven, 230°C (450°F), Gas Mark 8, for 15–20 minutes. If the rolls are cooked, they will sound hollow when tapped on the bottom (remember to pick them up with oven gloves as they will be hot). Transfer to a wire rack to cool.

For sweet bread roll snacks, add 250 g (8 oz) mixed dried fruit to the dry ingredients with 2 teaspoons ground cinnamon and 3 tablespoons caster sugar. Continue as above, shaping into 8 round balls and baking as above. Cool and serve either warm or cold, split and spread thinly with a little unsalted butter.

a very happy birthday cake

Serves **12**
Preparation time **25 minutes**
Cooking time **35–40 minutes**

175 g (6 oz) **soft margarine**, plus extra for greasing
175 g (6 oz) **caster sugar**
2 teaspoons **vanilla essence**
300 g (10 oz) **self-raising flour**
2 teaspoons **baking powder**
3 **eggs**
50 g (2 oz) **ground rice**
150 ml (¼ pint) **low-fat natural yogurt**
175 g (6 oz) **strawberries**, finely chopped
300 ml (½ pint) **double cream**
3 tablespoons **reduced-sugar strawberry jam**

Grease 2 x 20 cm (8 inch) loose-bottomed, round cake tins lightly with margarine, and line the bases of the tins with nonstick baking paper. Cream the margarine and sugar in a food processor with the vanilla essence until smooth.

Sift the flour and baking powder over the creamed mixture, add the eggs, ground rice and yogurt and whiz together until creamy. Fold the strawberries into the mixture.

Divide the mixture between the prepared tins and bake in a preheated oven, 180°C (350°F), Gas Mark 4, for 35–40 minutes until risen, golden and springy to the touch. Allow to cool in the tins for 10 minutes before removing to a wire rack to cool completely. Remove the baking paper.

Whisk the cream until soft peaks form. Cut the top off one of the cakes to level it, then spread with the jam and then half of the cream to the edges. Scatter with two-thirds of the strawberries. Place the other cake on top and spread with the remaining cream. Scatter with the remaining strawberries or form them into your child's initials. Add candles.

For chocolate birthday cake, replace 25 g (1 oz) of the flour with cocoa powder and bake as above. Omit the jam and simply fill with the cream. Replace the strawberries with 200 g (7 oz) chocolate-coated honeycomb balls, lightly crushed and used to fill and decorate the cake.

rudolph's santa snacks

Makes **about 14**
Preparation time **15 minutes**
Cooking time **15 minutes**

50 g (2 oz) **cornflakes**
100 g (3½ oz) **butter** or **margarine**, softened
75 g (3 oz) **caster sugar**
1 **egg yolk**
few drops **vanilla essence**
125 g (4 oz) **self-raising flour**
25 g (1 oz) **cornflour**
7 **glacé cherries**, sliced in half, to decorate

Place the cornflakes in a plastic bag. Crush them with your hands or bash them with a rolling pin, then tip on to a plate and set aside.

Put the butter and sugar into a mixing bowl and cream them together with a wooden spoon until pale and fluffy. Add the egg yolk and vanilla essence and stir in. Sift in the flour and cornflour and stir them into the mix.

Take walnut-sized amounts of the mixture and make them into about 14 balls. Roll the balls in the crushed cornflakes until covered, then place them on a baking sheet lined with nonstick baking paper, leaving plenty of space between them, and decorate the top of each one with half a glacé cherry.

Bake the biscuits in a preheated oven, 190°C (375°F), Gas Mark 5, for 15 minutes, or until a light golden brown, then remove from the oven and allow to cool a little before transferring to a wire cooling rack.

For Santa's chocolate snowy snacks, add 50 g (2 oz) plain chocolate drops to the mixture with the flour and cornflour, then add 1 tablespoon cocoa powder. Stir and then cook as above. Once cooked, dust with a little icing sugar to resemble snow.

melon & pineapple salad

Serves **4**
Preparation time **10 minutes**

½ **cantaloupe melon**, peeled, deseeded and diced
½ small **pineapple**, peeled and diced
finely grated rind of 1 **lime**
2 teaspoons **fructose**
quarter slices of **lime**, to decorate

Put the melon and pineapple in a bowl or plastic storage box.

Mix together the lime rind and fructose until well combined. Sprinkle over the fruit and mix together well – in 1 hour or so the fructose will have dissolved.

Decorate with the lime slices and serve.

For watermelon, pear & strawberry salad, cut ½ small watermelon into cubes and place in a plastic storage box. Toss with 2 peeled, cored and sliced pears and 175 g (6 oz) hulled and halved small strawberries. Mix with 3 tablespoons orange juice and decorate with orange or clementine slices.

blueberry & soft cheese traybake

Serves **12**
Preparation time **20 minutes**
Cooking time **20 minutes**

175 g (6 oz) **butter**, softened
75 g (3 oz) **soft brown sugar**
375 g (12 oz) **soft cheese**
2 teaspoons **vanilla essence**
3 **eggs**
175 g (6 oz) **plain flour**
175 g (6 oz) **wholemeal flour**
175 g (6 oz) **blueberries**
75 g (3 oz) **icing sugar**, sifted
½ teaspoon **ground cinnamon** (optional)

Grease a 28 x 18 cm (11 x 7 inch) deep Swiss roll tin lightly with butter and line the base with nonstick baking paper.

Place 150 g (5 oz) of the butter into a bowl and beat well until smooth with a wooden spoon. Add the sugar, 150 g (5 oz) of the soft cheese and the vanilla essence and beat again. Add the eggs and sift in the flours. Mix together to combine well.

Fold the blueberries into the cake mixture, then transfer to the prepared tin and level. Bake in a preheated oven, 180°C (350°F), Gas Mark 4, for 20 minutes until golden and firm to the touch. Allow to cool for 10 minutes in the tin before turning the cake out on to a wire rack to cool completely.

Beat together the remaining soft cheese and remaining butter with the icing sugar and half of the cinnamon, if using, and spread over the surface of the cake. Cut into 12 squares, then sprinkle with the remaining cinnamon, if liked.

For raspberry & orange traybake, add the grated rind of ½ orange to the creamed butter, sugar and soft cheese mixture, then replace the blueberries with 125 g (4 oz) raspberries, folding in very carefully so as not to break up the fruit. Bake as above, then make up the same topping, replacing the cinnamon with the remaining orange rind, and spread over the top.

cheesy twists

Makes **about 15**
Preparation time **15 minutes**
Cooking time **8–12 minutes**

50 g (2 oz) **Cheddar cheese**, grated 1/2 cup
75 g (3 oz) **self-raising flour**, plus extra for dusting 1/2 cup *
½ teaspoon **mustard powder**
50 g (2 oz) chilled **butter**, cut into cubes 1/4 cup
1 **egg yolk**

*(Add 1 tsp baking powder)

Put the Cheddar into a mixing bowl, then sift the flour and mustard powder into the bowl. Add the butter, then rub the cheese, butter and flour together until the butter is broken up and covered in flour and the mixture looks like fine breadcrumbs. Add the egg yolk to the mixture and stir with a wooden spoon until you have a stiff dough.

Roll out the dough on a well-floured surface until it is about 5 mm (¼ inch) thick. Take a sharp knife and cut the dough into about 15 long strips, about 1 cm (½ inch) thick. Pick up each strip carefully and twist it gently before laying it on a baking sheet lined with nonstick baking paper.

Bake the twists in a preheated oven, 220°C (425°F), Gas Mark 7, for 8–12 minutes until golden brown, then remove them from the oven and allow to cool on the baking sheet.

For spinach & Parmesan twists, place the flour in a food processor with a handful of spinach leaves and whiz until fine and green in colour. Add the remaining ingredients, replacing the Cheddar with freshly grated Parmesan, then continue as above.

grandma's courgette loaf

Serves **8–10**
Preparation time **30 minutes**
Cooking time **about 1 hour 15 minutes**

275 g (9 oz) **self-raising flour**
1 teaspoon **baking powder**
2 teaspoons **mixed spice**
2 **courgettes**, grated
125 g (4 oz) **soft brown sugar**
1 **egg**
75 ml (3 fl oz) **milk**
75 g (3 oz) **butter**, plus extra for greasing
75 g (3 oz) **raisins**
75 g (3 oz) **walnuts**, chopped

Topping
50 g (2 oz) **plain flour**
25 g (1 oz) **soft brown sugar**
½ teaspoon **mixed spice**
50 g (2 oz) chilled **butter**, cut into cubes
50 g (2 oz) **walnuts**, finely chopped

Grease a 1 kg (2 lb) loaf tin lightly with butter and line the base with nonstick baking paper. Sift the flour, baking powder and mixed spice into a large bowl and add the courgettes and sugar. Stir well.

Beat the egg and milk together in a jug. Melt the butter in a small pan, then add the raisins and stir well over a gentle heat for a few seconds to help plump them up. Pour the melted butter and milk and egg mixture into the dry ingredients and stir until well combined. Add the walnuts and stir again. Transfer to the prepared tin and level.

Make the streusel topping: mix the flour with the sugar and mixed spice, then rub the butter into the dry ingredients until the mixture resembles fine breadcrumbs. Stir in the walnuts, then scatter over the cake.

Bake the loaf in a preheated oven, 180°C (350°F), Gas Mark 4, for 1 hour to 1 hour 10 minutes until well risen and firm to the touch and a skewer inserted comes out clean. Allow it to cool for 10 minutes in the tin before turning out on to a wire rack to cool completely.

For moist mango loaf, replace the courgettes, raisins and walnuts with 200 ml (7 fl oz) mango purée, 1 teaspoon vanilla essence and ½ mango, roughly chopped, all folded into the wet mixture. Use the same streusel topping as above, but bake for 40–45 minutes until firm and well risen.

berried treasures

Serves **4**
Preparation time **15 minutes**
Cooking time **2 minutes**

125 g (4 oz) **white chocolate**, at room temperature
2 tablespoons **milk**
150 ml (¼ pint) **double cream**
150 g (5 oz) **blackberries**
1 tablespoon **clear honey**
1 **egg white**

Break off a quarter of the white chocolate. Using a potato peeler, shave off some chocolate curls to decorate the desserts.

Place the remaining pieces of chocolate in a small heatproof bowl. Add the milk and microwave on full power for 2 minutes. Leave to stand for 1 minute then stir. If lumps remain in the chocolate, microwave again for a further 30 seconds until melted. (Alternatively, put the chocolate and milk in a small heatproof bowl and rest it over a small saucepan of gently simmering water.) Stir in the cream and pour into a cool bowl, allow to cool completely, then put in the freezer for 5 minutes.

Reserve 4 blackberries and blend the remainder in a food processor with the honey until puréed. Turn into a fine-meshed sieve over a bowl and press the purée through with the back of a dessertspoon to extract the seeds.

Whisk the egg white until it stands in soft peaks when the whisk is lifted from the bowl.

Remove the chocolate cream from the freezer and whisk until it starts to thicken. This might take a few minutes. Gently stir in the egg white.

Spoon half the chocolate mixture into 4 small serving dishes or cups and spoon over the fruit purée. Top with the remaining chocolate mixture and give each a light stir with the handle end of a teaspoon so you can see a swirl of the blackberry purée. Decorate with the reserved berries and chocolate curls and chill until ready to serve.

granola squares

Makes **12**
Preparation time **15 minutes**, plus chilling
Cooking time **20 minutes**

175 g (6 oz) **butter**, plus extra for greasing
150 ml (¼ pint) **clear honey**
2 tablespoons **maple syrup**
1 teaspoon **ground cinnamon**
125 g (4 oz) ready-to-eat **dried apricots**, roughly chopped
100 g (4 oz) ready-to-eat **dried papaya** or **mango**, roughly chopped
125 g (4 oz) **raisins**
4 tablespoons **pumpkin seeds**
2 tablespoons **sesame seeds**
3 tablespoons **sunflower seeds**
75 g (3 oz) **pecan nuts**, roughly chopped
275 g (9 oz) **porridge oats**

Grease a 28 x 18 cm (11 x 7 inch) deep Swiss roll tin with butter and line the base with nonstick baking paper.

Place the butter, honey and maple syrup in a medium saucepan and heat, stirring continually, until the butter has melted. Add the cinnamon, dried fruit, seeds and nuts, stir the mixture and heat for 1 minute. Remove from the heat and add the porridge oats, stirring until they are well coated in the syrup.

Transfer the mixture to the prepared tin and smooth down with the back of a spoon to compact into the tin and level. Bake in a preheated oven, 180°C (350°F), Gas Mark 4, for 15 minutes until the top is just beginning to brown. Remove from the oven and allow to cool in the tin, then chill in the refrigerator for 30–60 minutes.

Turn out the chilled granola, upside down, on a chopping board, then carefully flip it back over to its correct side. Using a long, sharp knife (preferably longer than the granola itself), cut into 12 squares.

For fruity chocolate granola squares, leave out the pecans and seeds and replace with 75 g (3 oz) roughly chopped ready-to-eat dried apples. Once cooled, drizzle 50 g (2 oz) melted white chocolate over the top. Allow to set in the refrigerator for 10 minutes before cutting into squares.

choc-peanut cake

Makes a **1 kg (2 lb) loaf cake**
Preparation time **15 minutes**
Cooking time **about 1 hour**

125 g (4 oz) **plain flour**
50 g (2 oz) **wholemeal flour**
1 teaspoon **baking powder**
3 tablespoons **golden caster sugar**
100 g (3½ oz) **smooth peanut butter**
125 g (4 oz) **butter**, softened
3 **eggs**, lightly beaten
1 teaspoon **vanilla extract**
50 ml (2 fl oz) **apple juice**
100 g (3½ oz) **plain chocolate chips** or **plain dark chocolate**, chopped
1 large **dessert apple**, peeled, cored and chopped

Line a 1 kg (2 lb) loaf tin with nonstick baking paper. Sift the flours and baking powder into a large bowl. Mix in the sugar, peanut butter, butter, eggs, vanilla extract and apple juice. Stir through the chocolate chips and apple.

Spoon the mixture into the prepared tin and bake in a preheated oven, 180°C (350°F), Gas Mark 4, for 1 hour. To see if it is cooked, insert a skewer in the centre of the loaf – if it comes out clean it is done, but if cake mix is attached to the skewer it will need another 10 minutes.

Remove the cake from the oven and turn out on to a wire rack. Peel off the baking paper and leave to cool. Serve cut into slices.

For honey cake, replace the peanut butter with 125 g (4 oz) thick honey and omit the chocolate chips. Drizzle with 2 tablespoons clear honey before serving.

cherry, bran & raisin muffins

Makes **12**
Preparation time **15 minutes**
Cooking time **20–25 minutes**

125 g (4 oz) **oatbran**
250 g (8 oz) **self-raising flour**
1 teaspoon **baking powder**
1 teaspoon **bicarbonate of soda**
1 teaspoon **ground cinnamon**
½ teaspoon **ground ginger**
125 g (4 oz) **soft brown sugar**
1 **egg**
75 ml (3 fl oz) **vegetable oil**
100 ml (3½ fl oz) **milk**
250 g (8 oz) **cherries**, stoned and halved
125 g (4 oz) **raisins**

Topping
250 g (8 oz) **mascarpone cheese**
2 tablespoons **icing sugar**

To decorate
12 **cherries**
pinch of **ground cinnamon** (optional)

Place the oatbran in a bowl. Sift the flour, baking powder, bicarbonate of soda, cinnamon and ginger over the top and mix together. Add the sugar and stir well.

Mix together in a jug the egg, oil and milk, then pour into the dry ingredients with the cherries and raisins and stir until just mixed. Line a 12-hole muffin tray with 12 paper muffin cases and divide the mixture between them. Bake in a preheated oven, 180°C (350°F), Gas Mark 4, for 20–25 minutes until well risen and golden. Remove the muffins from the tin and place on a wire rack to cool.

Beat the mascarpone and icing sugar in a bowl, then spoon and swirl on top of each cooled muffin. Decorate each with a cherry and a sprinkling of cinnamon, if liked.

For carrot-cake muffins, omit the oatbran and increase the flour to 275 g (9 oz). Add 1 teaspoon mixed spice. Replace the cherries with 2 grated carrots and add 75 g (3 oz) roughly chopped walnuts or pecans. Bake as above, then decorate with the same topping and a walnut half instead of a cherry.

chocolate-toffee popcorn

Makes about **175 g (6 oz)**
Preparation time **15 minutes**
Cooking time **about 10 minutes**

about 50 g (2 oz) **milk chocolate**, broken into pieces
50 g (2 oz) **firm toffees**
4 tablespoons **milk**
1 tablespoon **vegetable oil**
75 g (3 oz) **popcorn kernels**

Place the chocolate pieces in a small heatproof bowl. Microwave on medium power for 1 minute. Leave to stand for 2 minutes, then microwave again for 30 seconds at a time until melted, stirring frequently to avoid lumps. (Alternatively, melt the chocolate carefully in a small heatproof bowl over a small saucepan of gently simmering water.)

Unwrap the toffees and put them in a polythene bag. Place on a chopping board and tap firmly with a rolling pin until the toffees have broken into small pieces. Tip the pieces into a small saucepan and add the milk. Cook on the lowest possible heat until the toffee has melted (this will take several minutes, depending on the firmness of the toffee). Remove from the heat.

Put the oil in a large saucepan with a tight-fitting lid and heat for 1 minute. Add the popcorn kernels and cover with the lid. Cook until the popping sound stops, then tip the corn out on to a large baking sheet or roasting tin and leave for 5 minutes.

Using a teaspoon, drizzle lines of the toffee sauce over the corn until lightly coated. Drizzle with lines of chocolate in the same way.

For golden-nugget popcorn, cook the popcorn kernels as above, but replace the remaining ingredients with 4 tablespoons golden syrup heated in a small pan with 25 g (1 oz) butter until melted, then add 50 g (2 oz) roughly chopped roasted cashews. Cool slightly then toss with the popcorn to coat lightly.

banana & chocolate loaf cake

Serves **8–10**
Preparation time **15 minutes**
Cooking time **55–60 minutes**

250 g (8 oz) **butter**, softened, plus extra for greasing
125 g (4 oz) **caster sugar**
1 teaspoon **vanilla extract**
3 **eggs**, beaten
300 g (10 oz) **self-raising flour**
1 teaspoon **baking powder**
3 ripe **bananas**, mashed
2 tablespoons **milk**
175 g (6 oz) **plain dark chocolate**, roughly chopped, or **chocolate chips**

Grease a 1 kg (2 lb) loaf tin lightly with butter and line the base with nonstick baking paper. Beat the butter, sugar and vanilla extract together in a bowl until smooth and creamy. Add the eggs and sift over the flour and baking powder. Beat together until smooth and creamy.

Add the bananas, milk and chopped chocolate and fold together until well mixed. Transfer the mixture to the prepared tin and bake in a preheated oven, 180°C (350°F), Gas Mark 4, for 55–60 minutes until the cake is well risen and golden.

Cool the cake in the tin for 10 minutes before turning out on to a wire rack to cool completely. Serve cut into slices.

For double-chocolate no-wheat banana loaf, replace the flour with 300 g (10 oz) rice flour and add 4 tablespoons of cocoa powder when sifting into the bowl.

vanilla flowers

Makes **30**
Preparation time **30 minutes**
Cooking time **10–15 minutes**

200 g (7 oz) **butter**, softened
few drops **vanilla essence**
50 g (2 oz) **icing sugar**
175 g (6 oz) **plain flour**
50 g (2 oz) **cornflour**
cake decorations, to decorate

Place the butter and vanilla essence in a mixing bowl and sift in the icing sugar. Cream the ingredients together with a wooden spoon. Sift in the flour and the cornflour a little at a time and fold in with a metal spoon.

Spoon the mixture into a piping bag, and pipe the mixture on to a baking sheet lined with nonstick baking paper, making little flower shapes. To finish a flower, push the nozzle down into the piped flower as you stop squeezing. Press a decoration into the centre of each one.

Bake the cookies in a preheated oven, 190°C (375°F), Gas Mark 5, for 10–15 minutes or until they are a pale golden colour. Remove from the oven and allow to cool for a few minutes on the baking sheet before transferring to a cooling rack.

For ginger flowers, mix 1 teaspoon ground allspice or mixed spice in with the cornflour. Decorate the centre of each with ¼ piece stem ginger before baking as above.

upside-down tarts

Serves **4**
Preparation time **10 minutes**
Cooking time **15–18 minutes**

25 g (1 oz) **unsalted butter**
25 g (1 oz) **light muscovado sugar**
50 g (2 oz) **redcurrants**
2 ripe **pears**, peeled, cored and cut into chunky pieces
½ x 375 g (12 oz) pack **ready-rolled puff pastry**, thawed if frozen and removed from the refrigerator

Thinly slice the butter and divide it among 4 small heatproof ramekin dishes. Sprinkle with the sugar. If the redcurrants are still attached to their stalks, reserve 4 clusters for decoration and remove the rest from the stalks (the easiest way to do this is to run the currants between the prongs of a fork). Scatter several redcurrants into each dish, then add the pears.

Unroll the pastry and cut out rounds using a 10 cm (4 inch) biscuit cutter. Lay the pastry rounds over the pears, tucking the edges down inside the dishes.

Place the dishes on a baking sheet and bake in a preheated oven, 220°C (425°F), Gas Mark 7, for 15–18 minutes or until the pastry is well risen and pale golden. Using oven gloves, remove the baking sheet from the oven and put it on a heatproof surface. Leave to cool slightly.

Loosen the edges of the pastry with a knife. Hold a ramekin dish with oven gloves and invert a small serving plate on top. Carefully flip over the dish and plate so that the plate is the right way up. Lift off the dish to reveal the tart with its fruity topping. Repeat with the remaining tarts. Serve decorated with the remaining redcurrants.

For banana & maple syrup upside-down tarts, replace the redcurrants and pears with 2 thinly sliced bananas, placing them in the bases of each of the buttered ramekins and drizzling each with 1 tablespoon maple syrup. Top with the pastry and bake as above.

pumpkin seed & fruit bars

Makes **8**
Preparation time **15 minutes**, plus chilling
Cooking time **5 minutes**

50 g (2 oz) **pumpkin seeds**
75 g (3 oz) **dried soya beans**
75 g (3 oz) **raisins**
75 g (3 oz) ready-to-eat **dried apricots**, roughly chopped
50 g (2 oz) **dried cranberries**
300 g (10 oz) **plain dark chocolate**, broken into pieces

Lightly grease a 28 x 18 cm (11 x 7 inch) Swiss roll tin and line the base with nonstick baking paper. Put the seeds, soya beans and all the fruit into a bowl.

Melt the chocolate (see page 180). Remove from the heat, pour over the seed and fruit mixture and stir well to coat completely.

Transfer the mixture to the prepared tin and level with the back of a spoon to fill the tin evenly. Chill in the refrigerator for 1 hour until set and firm. Cut into 8 bars and keep refrigerated in an airtight container until ready to use.

For yogurt-coated bars, replace the plain dark chocolate with 200 g (7 oz) white chocolate melted over simmering water. When melted, remove from the heat and add 2 tablespoons natural yogurt and ½ teaspoon vanilla essence. Stir well, then add to the dry ingredients and stir to coat. Transfer into the tin and chill as above.

christmas garlands

Makes **6**
Preparation time **30 minutes**
Cooking time **about 15 minutes**

50 g (2 oz) **butter**
150 g (5 oz) **plain flour**
50 g (2 oz) **caster sugar**, plus a little for sprinkling
finely grated rind of 1 small **lemon**
1 **egg**, beaten
pieces of **angelica and glacé cherries**, to decorate

Put the butter in a bowl, sift in the flour and rub together until the mixture resembles fine breadcrumbs. Add the sugar and lemon rind and stir everything together with a wooden spoon. Add most of the egg and stir again until the mixture comes together, then use your hands to draw the dough together into a ball.

Pick off small pieces of dough and roll them into balls, each about the size of a cherry. Press 8 balls of the cookie dough together into a circle, then repeat to make a further 5 garlands. Place small pieces of glacé cherry or angelica between the balls.

Place the garlands on a baking sheet lined with nonstick baking paper and bake in a preheated oven, 190°C (375°F), Gas Mark 5, for about 15 minutes or until pale golden. Just before the end of the cooking time, brush with the remainder of the egg and sprinkle with caster sugar, then return to the oven to finish cooking.

Remove from the oven and allow to cool a little before transferring to a cooling rack. Thread on to ribbons and use as decorations.

For Christmas trees, using 10 small balls of dough per tree, create Christmas tree shapes by starting with 1 as a top row, followed by 2, 3 and 4 on the bottom row. This will create a classic triangular Christmas tree shape. Decorate the trees with angelica and glacé cherries and bake as above.

chocolate scribble cake

Makes **9 squares**
Preparation time **15 minutes**
Cooking time **20 minutes**

50 g (2 oz) **plain dark chocolate**, broken into small pieces
½ cup 50 g (2 oz) **butter** or **margarine**
2 **eggs**
½ cup 150 g (5 oz) **light soft brown sugar**
¼ cup 50 g (2 oz) **self-raising flour**
icing pens, to decorate (optional)
~~1 tsp~~ ½ tsp B.P

Melt the chocolate together with the butter (see page 180).

Break the eggs into a mixing bowl, then add the sugar and sift in the flour. Stir them together vigorously.

Stir the melted chocolate and butter and carefully pour them into the mixing bowl. Stir the mixture until it is smooth, then pour into a shallow cake tin, 20 cm (8 inches) square, lined with nonstick baking paper, using the spatula to scrape every last bit from the bowl. Place on the top shelf of a preheated oven, 180°C (350°F), Gas Mark 4, for 20 minutes or until just firm when you touch it very gently in the middle.

Allow the cake to cool in the tin, then cut it into 9 pieces in the tin. Using the icing pens, decorate the squares with icing scribbles, if liked.

For pink coconut cake, make an all-in-one cake mix of 125 g (4 oz) self-raising flour, 125 g (4 oz) soft margarine, 125 g (4 oz) caster sugar and 2 eggs; beat together until smooth and creamy and then transfer to a 20 cm (8 inch) greased and base-lined square tin. Bake in the preheated oven as above for 20 minutes until golden and a skewer inserted comes out clean. Transfer to a wire rack to cool. Mix 75 g (3 oz) sifted icing sugar with 1–2 teaspoons beetroot juice until smooth and blended. Spread thinly over the cake and scatter with 1 tablespoon desiccated coconut. Cut into squares to serve.

desserts

multicoloured fresh fruit lollies

Serves **8**
Preparation time **20 minutes**, plus freezing
Cooking time **15 minutes**

300 g (10 oz) fresh **raspberries**
25 g (1 oz) **caster sugar**
150 ml (¼ pint) **water**, plus 4 tablespoons
400 g (13 oz) can **peaches** in natural juice

Place the raspberries and sugar in a small pan with 4 tablespoons of the measured water and bring to the boil, stirring well until the sugar dissolves. Add the remaining measured water.

Put the raspberry liquid through a sieve, pressing down well with a metal spoon to make as much of the pulp go through as possible, only discarding the seeds.

Pour the mixture into 8 lolly moulds, filling just the base of each. (Try using 8 rinsed yogurt pots placed in a roasting tin. Cover with foil and push lolly sticks through the foil into the centre of each pot. The foil will help secure the stick in the centre.) Freeze for 1–2 hours until firm.

Meanwhile, put the peaches and juice into a food processor and whiz until smooth. Once the raspberry base is firm, pour the peach liquid over the top of the raspberry mixture and freeze for a further 1–2 hours or overnight until firm.

For yogurt peach melba lollies, omit the sugar and water and whiz together the raspberries, peaches and 150 ml (¼ pint) raspberry-flavoured drinking yogurt in a food processor. Divide between 8 lolly moulds and freeze for 4–5 hours until firm.

sugared fruit pancakes

Makes **20–24**
Preparation time **15 minutes**
Cooking time **10 minutes**

2 **eggs**
25 g (1 oz) **unsalted butter**
100 ml (3½ fl oz) **milk**
100 g (3½ oz) **plain flour**
1 teaspoon **baking powder**
2 tablespoons **vanilla** or **caster sugar**
125 g (4 oz) **blueberries**
cooking oil, for frying

Separate the eggs into 2 bowls, egg yolks in one and egg whites in another. Put the butter in a heatproof bowl and heat in the microwave for 30 seconds until melted. Add the milk and pour the mixture over the egg yolks, stirring well.

Put the flour, baking powder and 1 tablespoon of the sugar in a large bowl. Add the milk mixture and whisk well to make a smooth batter. Stir in the blueberries.

Whisk the egg whites until they form firm peaks. Using a large metal spoon, gently fold the whites into the batter until well mixed.

Heat a little oil in a large frying pan for 1 minute. Add a dessertspoonful of the batter to one side of the pan so it spreads to make a little cake. Add 2–3 more spoonfuls, depending on the size of the pan, so the pancakes can cook without touching. When the pancakes are golden on the underside (check by lifting with a palette knife or fish slice), flip them over and cook again until golden. Remove the pancakes from the pan and transfer to a serving plate, then keep them warm while you cook the remainder.

Sprinkle with the remaining sugar and serve.

For vanilla & fig pancakes, add 1 teaspoon vanilla essence to the milk in the pancakes, omit the blueberries and make as above. Cut 3 small figs into wedges and place into a pan with 15 g (½ oz) unsalted butter and 3 tablespoons maple syrup and heat for 2 minutes, stirring until soft. Spoon over the warm pancakes and serve with the yogurt.

toffee peaches

Serves **4**
Preparation time **10 minutes**
Cooking time **15 minutes**

4 **peaches**, halved and stoned
50 g (2 oz) **ground almonds**

Sauce
125 (4 oz) **soft light brown sugar**
5 tablespoons **maple syrup**
25 g (1 oz) **butter**
150 ml (¼ pint) **single cream**

Cut 4 x 20 cm (8 inch) square pieces of foil and place 2 peach halves in each. Sprinkle over the ground almonds. Scrunch up the foil to form 4 parcels and place under a preheated medium grill or 5–8 minutes, turning once or twice during cooking until the peaches are soft.

Meanwhile, make the sauce. Place the sugar, maple syrup and butter in a nonstick saucepan over a moderately low heat until the sugar dissolves. Stir continuously until the sauce boils and thickens, which should take about 3 minutes. Add the cream and return to the boil, then immediately remove from the heat.

Drizzle the sauce over the peaches, and serve.

For toffee apples, place 4 halved apples in sheets of foil and divide 15 g (½ oz) butter between them in cubes, dotting over the top. Sprinkle with a little ground cinnamon and grill for 10–12 minutes until the apples have softened, yet still retain their shape. Serve with the sauce as above.

rainbow tart

Serves **8**
Preparation time **25 minutes**
Cooking time **30 minutes**

375 g (12 oz) packet **sweet pastry**
2 **egg yolks**
3 tablespoons **cornflour**
3 tablespoons **caster sugar**
300 ml (½ pint) **milk**
1 teaspoon **vanilla essence**
1 large **orange**, segmented
175 g (6 oz) **strawberries**, halved
125 g (4 oz) **blueberries**
2 thick fresh **pineapple** rings, cut into bite-sized chunks
2 **kiwifruits**, sliced
icing sugar, to dust
crème fraîche or **natural yogurt**, to serve

Line a 23 cm (9 inch) fluted flan tin with the pastry. Trim the edges, then press the pastry firmly into the grooves so the rim sits a little higher than the tin. Fill with scrunched-up nonstick baking paper and baking beans, then bake in a preheated oven, 180°C (350°F), Gas Mark 4, for 15 minutes. Remove the paper and beans and bake for a further 5 minutes. Set aside to cool.

Mix the egg yolks, cornflour and sugar in a bowl. Put the milk in a heavy-based nonstick pan and bring to the boil. Pour over the egg mixture and blend well using a balloon whisk. Add the vanilla essence, then return to the rinsed-out pan and bring to the boil, whisking continuously until boiled and thickened. Transfer to a bowl to cool, stirring occasionally. Cover with clingfilm to prevent a skin forming.

Place the cooled pastry case on a serving plate and fill with the custard using a metal spoon to swirl up to the rim. Put the fruit in a bowl and toss to mix, then loosely arrange over the top of the custard. Dust with icing sugar and serve in wedges with spoonfuls of crème fraîche or yogurt.

For sunshine tart, mix 2 segmented oranges, 3 thick slices fresh pineapple, cut into chunks, 2 bananas, cut into chunks and tossed in 2 tablespoons lemon or lime juice, and 1 small mango, cut into chunks. Toss together and use to fill as above.

fairy crumble

Serves **6**
Preparation time **20 minutes**
Cooking time **30 minutes**

500 g (1 lb) **strawberries**, hulled and halved
250 g (8 oz) **raspberries**
1 **orange**, peeled and segmented
4 tablespoons **caster sugar**
½ teaspoon **ground cinnamon**

Topping
250 g (8 oz) **plain flour**
125 g (4 oz) **butter**, chilled and cubed
75 g (3 oz) **soft brown sugar**
50 g (2 oz) toasted **hazelnuts**, roughly chopped, or **flaked almonds** (optional)

Custard
2 **egg yolks**
2 tablespoons **cornflour**
3 tablespoons **caster sugar**
350 ml (12 fl oz) **milk**
2 tablespoons **beetroot juice** (from a bought cooked-beetroot packet) or a drop of cochineal

Place the strawberries, raspberries, orange segments (plus any juice), sugar and cinnamon in a bowl and toss together gently to coat the fruit lightly in the sugar, taking care not to break up the raspberries. Transfer the fruit to a gratin dish and set aside while making the crumble topping.

Place the flour into a bowl and using your fingertips rub the butter into it until the mixture resembles fine breadcrumbs. Stir in the sugar and nuts, if using, then spoon the crumble over the top of the fruit. Bake in a preheated oven, 200°C (400°F), Gas Mark 6, for 25–30 minutes until the topping is golden and crisp in places.

Make the pink custard: place the egg yolks, cornflour and sugar in a bowl and blend together well. Put the milk in a heavy-based nonstick saucepan and bring to the boil. Pour the milk over the egg mixture, add the beetroot juice and whisk together well. Return to the heat and cook gently, stirring continuously until thickened.

Serve the crumble in bowls with the pink custard to spoon over.

For Caribbean-style crumble, replace the red berries with 1 large mango, cut into chunks, and 6 thick slices fresh pineapple, cut into chunks. Toss with the orange and 75 g (3 oz) raisins. Replace the nuts with 4 tablespoons desiccated coconut in the crumble. Serve with ice cream rather than custard.

blueberry & peach pudding

Serves **4**
Preparation time **20 minutes**
Cooking time **40 minutes**

3 **eggs**
150 g (5 oz) **plain flour**
125 g (4 oz) **icing sugar**, plus extra to dust
300 ml (½ pint) **milk**
1 teaspoon **vanilla essence**
15 g (½ oz) **butter**, softened
2 **peaches**, halved, stoned and cut into wedges
125 g (4 oz) **blueberries**
finely grated zest of 1 **lemon**

Beat the eggs, flour, sugar, milk and vanilla essence in a bowl until thick and creamy. Heavily grease a 20 cm (8 inch) round tin or ovenproof dish with the butter and arrange the peaches and blueberries inside. Sprinkle over the lemon zest.

Pour the batter over the fruit and bake in a preheated oven, 190°C (375°F), Gas Mark 5, for 35 minutes until the batter is firm.

Dust with icing sugar and serve warm in wedges.

For strawberry, banana & cherry pudding, replace the peaches and blueberries with 1 large banana, sliced into chunks, 175 g (6 oz) strawberries and 125 g (4 oz) fresh pitted cherries. Try adding 1 teaspoon of ground cinnamon to the fruit and toss if liked.

star-of-the-day dessert

Serves **6**
Preparation time **20 minutes**, plus chilling
Cooking time **3 minutes**

125 g (4 oz) ready-to-eat **dried prunes**, roughly chopped
150 ml (¼ pint) **water**
125 g (4 oz) **plain dark chocolate** (70% cocoa solids), broken into pieces
500 ml (17 fl oz) **natural yogurt**
25 g (1 oz) **milk or plain dark chocolate**, made into shavings, to decorate

Place the prunes in a pan with the measured water and bring to the boil. Immediately remove from the heat, transfer to a food processor and whiz until completely smooth.

Return the prunes to the pan with the chocolate pieces and heat over a very gentle heat, stirring continuously until the chocolate has melted. Remove from the heat and beat in the yogurt. Allow to cool.

Divide the dessert between 4 serving glasses and decorate with the chocolate shavings. Chill for about 30 minutes and serve.

For minted chocolate star-of-the-day dessert, use a mint-flavoured chocolate (70% cocoa solids), dust the tops with a little organic cocoa powder and serve with mint-chocolate sticks for a real treat.

soft-cooked bananas & yogurt ice

Serves **4**
Preparation time **20 minutes**, plus freezing
Cooking time **10 minutes**

3 tablespoons **caster sugar**
150 ml (¼ pint) **water**
2 x 500 ml (17 fl oz) pots **natural yogurt**
3 teaspoons **vanilla essence**
15 g (½ oz) **butter**, softened
4 ripe **bananas**
½ teaspoon **ground cinnamon** or **nutmeg** (optional)

To serve
4 tablespoons **maple syrup**
50 g (2 oz) broken **pecan nuts**

Place the sugar and measured water in a heavy-based saucepan and bring to the boil. Continue to boil for 3–5 minutes until the syrup has reduced by half. Remove from the heat and stir in the yogurt and vanilla essence. Transfer to a freezerproof container and freeze for 3 hours.

Remove the ice from the freezer and beat with a wooden spoon until slushy. Freeze for a further 4 hours, or overnight, until firm.

Heat the butter in a large nonstick frying pan. Halve the bananas lengthways, then cut each of the halves in half again across its width. Sprinkle the bananas, cut side up, with the spice, if using, and cook in the hot butter for 30–60 seconds on each side until golden. Remove from the pan using a slotted spoon.

Pile the bananas on to serving plates in a lattice pattern, then drizzle with the maple syrup and scatter with the pecans. Serve with scoops of the vanilla yogurt ice on top.

For strawberry yogurt ice, to serve as an alternative accompaniment, make as above, replacing the natural yogurt with a strawberry yogurt. Cook 375 g (12 oz) halved strawberries with ½ teaspoon freshly grated orange zest and 1 tablespoon maple syrup in the butter for 2–3 minutes until soft yet retaining their shape. Serve the warm strawberries with the strawberry yogurt ice.

sticky fig & banana traybake

Serves **6**
Preparation time **10 minutes**
Cooking time **20 minutes**

125 g (4 oz) **margarine** or **butter**, softened
125 g (4 oz) **soft brown sugar**
1 teaspoon **ground ginger**
2 **eggs**
125 g (4 oz) **plain flour**
3 **figs**, quartered
1 large **banana**, cut into chunks
2 tablespoons **maple syrup**
ice cream or **vanilla custard**, to serve

Beat the margarine or butter and sugar until smooth and creamy. Add the ginger, eggs and flour and beat again until a smooth mixture is formed. Lightly grease a 23 cm (9 inch) square tin or ovenproof dish, then spoon in the mixture and level with the back of a spoon.

Toss the figs and banana with the maple syrup and arrange over the top of the cake, pressing the fruit into the cake in places. Bake in a preheated oven, 180°C (350°F), Gas Mark 4, for 20 minutes until the cake is well risen and golden and the fruit is soft.

Serve the cake in squares with either scoops of ice cream or vanilla custard (see below).

For vanilla custard to serve as an accompaniment, heat 300 ml (½ pint) milk, with the seeds of ½ vanilla pod scraped into it, in a nonstick pan until boiling. Meanwhile, blend 2 egg yolks with 1 teaspoon cornflour and 2 tablespoons caster sugar. Pour the milk over the egg mixture once boiled and whisk well to blend. Return to the heat, stirring continuously until just beginning to boil and thicken. It will coat the back of a spoon.

end-of-summer custard pie

Serves **6–8**
Preparation time **20 minutes**, plus chilling
Cooking time **25 minutes**

150 g (5 oz) **plain flour**, plus extra for dusting
3 tablespoons **custard powder**
2 tablespoons **icing sugar**
75 g (3 oz) **butter**, chilled and cut into cubes
2–3 tablespoons **cold water**
500 g (1 lb) **blackberries**
2 **apples**, peeled, cored and roughly chopped
4 tablespoons **caster sugar**
1 tablespoon **clear honey**
beaten **egg**
vanilla ice cream (optional) or **crème fraîche** (optional), to serve

Sift the flour, custard powder and icing sugar into a bowl. Rub the butter using your fingertips into the flour until the mixture resembles fine breadcrumbs. Sprinkle over the measured water, then using a round-bladed knife begin to work the mixture into a smooth, firm dough. Wrap and chill for 15 minutes.

Toss the blackberries and apples with the sugar and honey and place in a 20 cm (8 inch) round pie dish or ovenproof dish.

Roll out the pastry, on a well-floured surface, to a round slightly larger than the pie dish. Place the dish on the pastry and cut around it using a sharp knife to produce a circle the correct size for the top. Using the pastry trimmings, make a border strip about 1 cm (½ inch) wide. Dampen the edges of the pie dish and fit the strips of pastry around the edge, pressing firmly. Dampen this pastry too before placing the circle on top and pressing again firmly to hold in place. Using any remaining trimmings, decorate the pie with leaves, flowers, birds or other shapes.

Brush with beaten egg to glaze and bake in a preheated oven, 200°C (400°F), Gas Mark 6, for 20–25 minutes until golden and crisp. Serve with vanilla ice cream or crème fraîche, if liked.

For cinnamon & peach custard pie, drain 2 x 400 g (13 oz) cans of peaches in natural juice and toss with the apples, 1 tablespoon soft brown sugar and 1 teaspoon ground cinnamon. Use instead of the blackberries with the custard pastry as above.

spider's web pancakes

Serves **8**
Preparation time **15 minutes**
Cooking time **15–20 minutes**

2 **eggs**
150 g (5 oz) **plain flour**
1 teaspoon **caster sugar**
300 ml (½ pint) **milk**
15 g (½ oz) **butter**, melted
300 ml (½ pint) **double cream**
3 teaspoons **clear honey**
250 g (8 oz) **raspberries**
vegetable oil, for frying
icing sugar, to dust

Whisk the eggs, flour and sugar in a bowl until well combined, then whisk in the milk until you have a smooth batter. Whisk in the melted butter, then set the batter aside.

Whip the cream very lightly until just beginning to peak, then fold in the honey and raspberries and chill whilst making the pancakes.

Heat a few drops of oil in a small, nonstick frying pan. Transfer the batter to a jug with a narrow spout, and pour a very thin stream of the batter, starting in the centre of the pan and continuing in continuous circles around, then across the pan to form a small web pattern about 15 cm (6 inches) in diameter. Cook for about 1 minute until set, then, using a fish slice, flip the pancake over and cook the other side for 30 seconds. Repeat to make 8 pancakes, stacking them between sheets of nonstick baking paper to keep warm.

Serve the warm pancakes filled with a little raspberry cream and dusted with icing sugar.

For apple & cinnamon spider's web pancakes, place 2 large peeled, cored and roughly chopped cooking apples in a pan with 3 tablespoons sultanas, 3 tablespoons water, ½ teaspoon ground cinnamon and 2 tablespoons soft brown sugar. Cook over a gentle heat for 3–5 minutes, stirring continuously until soft and pulpy. Remove from the heat and allow to cool. Serve folded into the cream as above, replacing the raspberries, or fill the pancakes with the apple mixture alone and serve with yogurt.

no-sugar brownies with berries

Serves **12**
Preparation time **20 minutes**
Cooking time **30 minutes**

250 g (8 oz) **plain dark chocolate** (70% cocoa solids)
½ cup 125 g (4 oz) **unsalted butter**
4 **eggs**
½ cup 150 g (5 oz) **plain flour**
¼ cup 50 g (2 oz) **ground almonds**
75 g (3 oz) **plain dark chocolate chips**
50 g (2 oz) **pecan nuts**, roughly chopped (optional)

To serve
fresh **blueberries, raspberries** and **strawberries**
ice cream or **crème fraîche**

Lightly grease a 28 x 18 cm (11 x 7 inch) baking tin and line the base with nonstick baking paper.

Melt the chocolate together with the butter (see page 180). Remove from the heat and allow to cool for 2 minutes. Whisk the eggs in a separate bowl until frothy (about 3 minutes), then stir in the cooled chocolate mixture.

Fold in the flour, ground almonds, chocolate chips and pecans, if using. Transfer to the prepared baking tin and bake in a preheated oven, 180°C (350°F), Gas Mark 4, for 25–30 minutes until just firm to the touch.

Leave the brownies to cool in the tin for 20 minutes before cutting into 12 squares and serving with the fresh berries and ice cream or crème fraîche.

For white chocolate & strawberry brownies (containing sugar in the chocolate), replace the plain dark chocolate with white chocolate, and the chocolate chips and pecans with 125 g (4 oz) finely chopped strawberries. This brownie will be soft and will only keep in the refrigerator for 3 days.

fruity refreshers

fresh lemonade

Makes **1.8 litres (3 pints)**
Preparation time **4–5 minutes**, plus cooling
Cooking time **4–5 minutes**

75 g (3 oz) **caster sugar**
1.8 litres (3 pints) **water**
4 **lemons**, sliced, plus extra slices to serve
ice cubes

Place the sugar in a pan with 600 ml (1 pint) of the measured water and all the sliced lemons. Bring to the boil, stirring well until all the sugar has dissolved.

Remove from the heat and add all the remaining water. Stir, then set aside to cool completely.

Once cold, roughly crush the lemons, to release all the juice. Strain through a sieve, add the ice cubes, and serve in glasses decorated with slices of lemon.

For fresh limeade, simply use 6 limes instead of 4 lemons, or use a mixture of the two. Try chopping the mint and adding while the limeade cools for a more intense mint flavour. Strain as above.

mango, melon & orange juice

Makes **about 400 ml (14 fl oz)**
Preparation time **5–6 minutes**

1 ripe **mango**, roughly chopped
½ **Galia melon**, deseeded and roughly chopped
200 ml (7 fl oz) **orange juice**
2 **ice cubes**

Place the mango and melon in a blender and whiz until smooth.

Add the orange juice and ice cubes, then purée until smooth. Serve immediately.

For coconut & pineapple juice, place 1 x 400 g (13 oz) can coconut milk in a food processor with ½ small pineapple, peeled, cored and roughly chopped. Whiz until smooth, then serve poured over ice and decorated with fresh cherries or strawberries for colour.

strawberry & vanilla milkshake

Serves **2**
Preparation time **5–6 minutes**, plus cooling
Cooking time **5–6 minutes**

300 ml (½ pint) **milk**
300 ml (½ pint) **single cream**
½ **vanilla pod**
250 g (8 oz) **strawberries**, hulled

Put the milk and cream in a pan. Remove the vanilla seeds from the pod using the back of a teaspoon and place the pod and seeds in the pan with the milk and cream. Bring to the boil, stirring. Once boiling point has been reached, remove from the heat and allow to cool completely.

Place the strawberries in a food processor and whiz until smooth. Add the cooled vanilla milk and whiz again until pink. Pour into chilled glasses and serve with straws.

For strawberry & vanilla ice cream milkshake, put the milk and strawberries in a food processor with 5 scoops of good-quality vanilla ice cream (the variety with vanilla seeds within the ice cream) and whiz until smooth and blended. Add some ice and whiz again. Pour into chilled glasses and serve.

watermelon & raspberry juice

Makes **about 200 ml (7 fl oz)**
Preparation time **5–6 minutes**

300 g (10 oz) **watermelon** (¼ an average fruit), deseeded and chopped
125 g (4 oz) **raspberries**
ice cubes, crushed (optional)

Put the watermelon and raspberries in a blender and whiz until smooth. Press the juice through a sieve to remove any raspberry pips.

Pour the juice into glasses over some crushed ice cubes, if liked.

For melon & apple juice, place half a small, deseeded and chopped, green melon into a food processor with 1 green apple, cored and cut into wedges (keep the skin on). Add 1 tablespoon lemon juice and whiz until smooth. Pour over crushed ice if liked.

nectarine & raspberry yogurt ice

Serves **2**
Preparation time **5 minutes**

3 ripe **nectarines**, halved and stoned
175 g (6 oz) **raspberries**
150 ml (¼ pint) **natural yogurt**
handful of **ice cubes**

Put the nectarines and raspberries in a food processor and whiz until really smooth. Add the yogurt and whiz again, then add the ice and whiz until very crushed and the shake thickens.

Pour into chilled glasses. Decorate with cocktail umbrellas and anything else to make the drink look fun!

For banana & mango coconut ice, replace the nectarines and raspberries with 1 large ripe banana and 1 mango, cut into chunks, and whiz until smooth. Add 150 ml (¼ pint) coconut milk and whiz again. Add the ice and whiz until the shake thickens. Pour into chilled glasses to serve.

peach, apple & strawberry lollies

Makes **4**
Preparation time **7–8 minutes**, plus freezing

2 **peaches**, peeled, stoned and cut into chunks
300 ml (½ pint) **water**
1 **red apple**, peeled
125 g (4 oz) **strawberries**, hulled

Place the peaches in a blender and whiz until smooth. Add one-third of the measured water and divide evenly between 4 lolly moulds. Freeze until just set.

Chop the apples into even-sized chunks and juice them. Add one-third of the water and pour on top of the frozen peach mixture, then freeze until just set.

Hull the strawberries and juice them. Add the remainder of the water and pour on top of the frozen apple mixture, then freeze until set.

For chocolate & orange lollies, place 1 x 300 g (10 oz) can mandarin segments in a food processor and whiz until smooth. Place into a pan with 125 g (4 oz) organic plain 70 per cent cocoa solids chocolate and gently heat until the chocolate has melted. Stir well with the orange pureé and pour into 4 lolly moulds. Freeze for 2 hours until firm.

traffic-light smoothie

Makes **400 ml (14 fl oz)**
Preparation time **9–10 minutes**

3 **kiwifruits**, roughly chopped
150 ml (¼ pint) **tangy-flavoured yogurt** (such as lemon or orange)
1 small **mango**, roughly chopped
2 tablespoons **orange** or **apple juice**
150 g (5 oz) **raspberries**
1–2 teaspoons **clear honey**

Whiz the kiwifruits in a blender until smooth and spoon the mixture into 2 tall glasses. Top each with a spoonful of yogurt, spreading the yogurt to the sides of the glasses.

Blend the mango to a purée with the orange or apple juice and spoon into the glasses. Top with another layer of yogurt.

Whiz the raspberries and push through a sieve over a bowl to extract the seeds. Check their sweetness (you might need to stir in a little honey if they are very sharp). Spoon the raspberry purée into glasses to serve.

For zebra layered blackberry smoothie, place 175 g (6 oz) blackberries into a food processor with 2 tablespoons clear honey and whiz until smooth. Layer alternatively with the yogurt to replace the kiwi, mango and orange juice.

index

almonds: crunchy honey yogurt 28
amber crumble 34
apples: apple & cinnamon spider's web pancakes 216
breakfast crumble 34
end-of-summer custard pie 214
melon & apple juice 228
peach, apple & strawberry lollies 232
toffee-apple porridge 18
toffee apples 200
apricots: amber crumble 34
granola squares 174
Asian noodles 90
asparagus: asparagus in blankets 58
beef & asparagus bagels 48
cheesy pizza-style worms 58
smoked salmon & asparagus bagels 48
aubergine & macaroni cheese 94
avocados: creamy avocado dip 46
guacamole 150

bacon: cheese & bacon pastries 152
chicken & bacon wraps 130
egg & bacon scone pizzas 118
green bean & bacon frittata 132
herby beans & bacon 24
late great breakfast 20
mushroom & bacon frittata 132
potato, bacon & tomato röstis 86
red lentil & bacon soup 50
rösti with bacon & eggs 92
bagels: beef & asparagus bagels 48
smoked salmon & asparagus bagels 48
bananas: banana & choc wholemeal muffins 30
banana & chocolate loaf cake 182
banana & mango coconut ice 230
banana & maple syrup upside-down tarts 186
banana & raisin flapjacks 156
breakfast smoothies 32
creamy banana pancakes 16
double-chocolate no-wheat banana loaf 182
soft-cooked bananas & yogurt ice 210
sticky fig & banana traybake 212
strawberry, banana & cherry pudding 206
beans: bean, coconut & spinach soup 50
beanfeast 44
herby beans & bacon 24
sausage & beans 24
tuna, bean & black olive salad 126
beef: Asian noodles with beef & coconut 90
beef & asparagus bagels 48
beef fajitas 150
mini steak burgers 142
spaghetti bolognaise 84
beetroot: hummus, pockets with 42
berried treasures 172
birthday cake 160
biscuits: cheesy twists 168
Christmas garlands 190
Christmas trees 190
ginger flowers 184
Rudolph's Santa snacks 162
Santa's chocolate snowy snacks 162
spinach & Parmesan twists 168
vanilla flowers 184
blackberries: berried treasures 172
end-of-summer custard pie 214
blueberries: blueberry & peach pudding 206
blueberry & soft cheese traybake 166
French toast with blueberries 22
sugared fruit pancakes 198
bolognaise pasta bake 84
bread: bread monsters 158
cheesy onion rolls 64
supper in a hurry 104
sweet bread roll snacks 158
tomato-garlic bread with ham 54
tuna melts 70
warm seedy rolls 64
see also toast
breadsticks 46
breakfast 8-9, 16-37
breakfast crumble 34
breakfast smoothies 32
brownies: no-sugar brownies with berries 218
white chocolate & strawberry brownies 218
bulgar wheat: chickpea & herb salad 126
burgers: mini steak 142
pork & apple 142
sausage & pepper 120
vegetable 120
butternut squash *see* squash

cabbage: baked cabbage with nuts & cheese 102
coleslaw 56
cakes: banana & chocolate loaf cake 182
blueberry & soft cheese traybake 166
choc-peanut cake 176
chocolate birthday cake 160
chocolate scribble cake 192
double-chocolate no-wheat banana loaf 182
fruity chocolate granola squares 174
Grandma's courgette loaf 170
granola squares 174
honey cake 176
moist mango loaf 170
pink coconut cake 192
raspberry & orange traybakes 166
sticky fig & banana traybake 212
a very happy birthday cake 160
calzones: butternut squash & feta cheese 116
no-mess cheesy pepperoni 116
Caribbean-style crumble 204
carrot-cake muffins 178
cheese: baked cabbage with nuts & cheese 102
butternut squash & feta cheese calzones 116
cheese & bacon pastries 152
cheesy eggs & cress 40
cheesy onion rolls 64
cheesy pizza-style worms 58
cheesy red dip with breadsticks 46
cheesy tuna & prawn pie 88
cheesy twists 168
crumb-topped aubergine & macaroni cheese 94
crumb-topped macaroni cheese 94
green cheese pasta 78
haloumi & tomato pastries 152
ham & fresh pineapple pizza 138
lentil & paneer feast 44
melting mushrooms 36
mini quiches 114
mini scone pizzas 118
no-mess cheesy pepperoni calzones 116

pesto cheese wraps 74
potato & cheese röstis 86
root vegetable bake with nuts & cheese 102
supper in a hurry 104
tomato-garlic bread 54
tuna melts 70
warm haloumi & vegetable melts 70
cherries: cherry, bran & raisin muffins 178
fresh cherry & vanilla muffins 30
chicken: all-in-one chicken pie 100
chicken & bacon wraps 130
chicken & chorizo pizza 138
chicken & pea risotto 106
chicken fajitas & no-chilli salsa 150
chicken, pea & mint couscous 60
chicken rice salad 80
chicken satay skewers 140
lightly spiced chicken nuggets 136
mild chicken & squash curry 96
pan-fried chicken wraps 56
supper in a hurry 104
chickpeas: chickpea & herb salad 126
hummus pitta pockets 42
vegetable burgers 120
Chinese-style pork & pak choi wraps 62
Chinese-style turkey wraps 62
chips: fish & chips in paper cones 148
multicoloured root chips 122
chocolate: banana & choc wholemeal muffins 30
banana & chocolate loaf cake 182
berried treasures 172
choc-peanut cake 176
chocolate & orange lollies 232
chocolate birthday cake 160
chocolate scribble cake 192
chocolate-toffee popcorn 180
double-chocolate no-wheat banana loaf 182
fruity chocolate granola squares 174
minted chocolate star-of-the-day dessert 208
no-sugar brownies with berries 218
pumpkin seed & fruit bars 188
Santa's chocolate snowy snacks 162
star-of-the-day dessert 208
white chocolate & strawberry brownies 218
yogurt-coated bars 188
yogurt-coated cereal topping 28
chorizo: chicken & chorizo pizza 138
meaty chorizo Spanish tortilla 112
no-mess cheesy pepperoni calzones 116
spicy chorizo wrap 74
Christmas garlands 190
Christmas trees 190
cinnamon & peach custard pie 214
coconut cake, pink 192
coconut milk: banana & mango coconut ice 230
bean, coconut & spinach soup 50
coconut & pineapple juice 224
cod: sweet potato-topped fish pie 88
coleslaw 56
tuna & coleslaw wraps 130
cornflakes: Rudolph's Santa snacks 162
Santa's chocolate snowy snacks 162
yogurt-coated cereal topping 28
courgettes: courgette & garlic pasta 78
Grandma's courgette loaf 170
minted courgette fritters 128
warm haloumi & vegetable melts 70
couscous: chicken, pea & mint 60
jewelled 60
roasted vegetable 66
crumbles: amber 34
breakfast 34
Caribbean-style 204
fairy 204
cucumber: creamy cucumber & garlic dip 52
cucumber & sweetcorn salsa 146
curries: korma-style curried prawns 96
mild chicken & squash curry 96
custard 204, 212

desserts 11, 194-219
dinners 9, 76-107
dips: cheesy red dip with breadsticks 46
creamy avocado dip 46
creamy cucumber & garlic dip 52
lemony mayonnaise dip 148
sunset wedges & soured cream 52
tomato dip 128
dried fruit: pumpkin seed & fruit bars 188
sweet bread roll snacks 158
drinks 220-35
breakfast smoothies 32
coconut & pineapple juice 224
fresh lemonade 222
fresh limeade 222
mango, melon & orange juice 224
melon & apple juice 228
strawberry & vanilla ice cream milkshake 226
strawberry & vanilla milkshake 226
traffic-light smoothie 234
watermelon & raspberry juice 228
duck: Peking wraps 68
dumplings 98

eggs: cheesy eggs & cress 40
egg & bacon scone pizzas 118
egg-topped melting mushrooms 36
green bean & bacon frittata 132
late great breakfast 20
mushroom & bacon frittata 132
rösti with bacon & eggs 92
Spanish tortilla 112
traffic-light scrambled eggs 40
end-of-summer custard pie 214

fairy crumble 204
figs: sticky fig & banana traybake 212
vanilla & fig pancakes 198
fish & chips in paper cones 148
flapjacks: banana & raisin 156
ginger 156
French toast with blackberries 22
frittata: green bean & bacon 132
mushroom & bacon 132
fritters: minted courgette 128
sweetcorn 128
fruit: rainbow tart 202
sunshine tart 202
fruity chocolate granola squares 174

gammon: creamy chunky gammon pie 100
maple-glazed gammon wraps 56
ginger: ginger flapjacks 156
ginger flowers 184
Grandma's courgette loaf 170
granola squares 174
green bean & bacon frittata 132
guacamole 150

ham: asparagus in blankets 58
cheesy pizza-style worms 58
ham & fresh pineapple pizza 138
mini quiches 114
mini scone pizzas 118
tomato-garlic bread with ham 54
honey cake 176
hotpot with dumplings 98
hummus: crispy lamb Moroccan rolls 124
hummus pitta pockets 42
pockets with beetroot hummus 42

ice cream: banana & mango coconut ice 230
nectarine & raspberry yogurt ice 230
strawberry & vanilla ice cream milkshake 226
strawberry yogurt ice 210
yogurt ice 210

jewelled couscous 60

ketchup, tomato 26
kiwifruit: traffic-light smoothie 234
korma-style curried prawns 96

lamb: crispy lamb & lettuce Peking wraps 68
crispy lamb Moroccan rolls 124
lamb hotpot with dumplings 98
lamb kofta 124
tasty teatime pasties 110
late great breakfast 20
lemonade 222
lentils: lentil & paneer feast 44
red lentil & bacon soup 50
limeade 222
lollies: chocolate & orange 232
multicoloured fresh fruit 196
peach, apple & strawberry 232
yogurt peach melba 196
lunches 9, 38-75

macaroni: bolognaise pasta bake 84
crumb-topped aubergine & macaroni cheese 94
crumb-topped macaroni cheese 94
mangoes: banana & mango coconut ice 230
Caribbean-style crumble 204
mango, melon & orange juice 224
moist mango loaf 170
traffic-light smoothie 234
maple-glazed gammon wraps 56
mayonnaise 122
cheese & chive 122
lemony dip 148
melon: mango, melon & orange juice 224
melon & apple juice 228
melon & pineapple salad 164
milk: breakfast smoothies 32
strawberry & vanilla milkshake 226
minted chocolate star-of-the-day dessert 208
muffins: banana & choc wholemeal 30
carrot-cake 178
cherry, bran & raisin 178
fresh cherry & vanilla 30
morning muffins & tomato ketchup 26
tomato & mushroom 26
mushrooms: baked sweet potatoes & creamy mushrooms 72
egg-topped melting mushrooms 36
late great breakfast 20
melting mushrooms 36
mushroom & bacon frittata 132
tomato & mushroom muffins 26

naan breads: crispy lamb Moroccan rolls 124
nectarine & raspberry yogurt ice 230
no-sugar brownies with berries 218
noodles: Asian noodles with beef & coconut 90
Asian noodles with prawns 90
sweet & sour pork noodles 144

oats: banana & raisin flapjacks 156
crunchy honey yogurt 28
ginger flapjacks 156
granola squares 174
hot-pink porridge 18
toffee-apple porridge 18
oranges: chocolate & orange lollies 232
mango, melon & orange juice 224

pak choi: Chinese-style pork & pak choi wraps 62
pancakes: creamy banana 16
hot peach & cinnamon 16
spider's web 216
sugared fruit 198
vanilla & fig 198
paneer: lentil & paneer feast 44
parsnips: multicoloured root chips 122
root vegetable bake with nuts & cheese 102
pasta: bolognaise pasta bake 84
courgette & garlic pasta 78
crumb-topped aubergine & macaroni cheese 94
crumb-topped macaroni cheese 94
green cheese pasta 78
salmon pasta bake 82
spaghetti bolognaise 84
tuna pasta bake with sweetcorn 82
pastries: butternut squash & feta cheese calzones 116
cheese & bacon pastries 152
haloumi & tomato pastries 152
late great breakfast 20
no-mess cheesy pepperoni calzones 116
sausage & tomato pasties 20
tasty teatime pasties 110
see also pies
peaches: amber crumble 34
blueberry & peach pudding 206
cinnamon & peach custard pie 214
hot peach & cinnamon pancakes 16
multicoloured fresh fruit lollies 196
peach, apple & strawberry lollies 232
toffee peaches 200
yogurt peach melba lollies 196
peanut butter: choc-peanut cake 176
peanut-butter smoothies 32
peanuts: baked cabbage with nuts & cheese 102

pears: upside-down tarts 186
watermelon, pear & strawberry salad 164
peas: chicken & pea risotto 106
Peking wraps 68
peppers: cheesy red dip with breadsticks 46
late great breakfast 20
no-mess cheesy pepperoni calzones 116
red pepper, garlic & Parmesan quiches 114
sausage & pepper burgers 120
traffic-light scrambled eggs 40
warm haloumi & vegetable melts 70
pesto cheese wraps 74
pies: all-in-one chicken pie 100
cheesy tuna & prawn pie 88
cinnamon & peach custard pie 214
creamy chunky gammon pie 100
end-of-summer custard pie 214
sweet potato-topped fish pie 88
see also pastries
pineapple: Caribbean-style crumble 204
coconut & pineapple juice 224
ham & fresh pineapple pizza 138
melon & pineapple salad 164
pitta pockets, hummus 42
pizzas: chicken & chorizo 138
egg & bacon scone 118
ham & fresh pineapple 138
mini scone 118
popcorn: chocolate-toffee 180
golden-nugget 180
pork: Chinese-style pork & pak choi wraps 62
pork & apple burgers 142
pork satay skewers 140
speedy breaded pork escalopes 104
sweet & sour pork noodles 144
porridge: hot-pink 18
toffee-apple 18
potatoes: fish & chips in paper cones 148
multicoloured root chips 122
potato & cheese röstis 86
potato, bacon & tomato röstis 86
salmon rösti cakes 92
Spanish tortilla 112
sunset wedges & soured cream 52
prawns: Asian noodles with prawns 90
baked sweet potatoes & prawns 72
cheesy tuna & prawn pie 88
korma-style curried prawns 96
prawn rice salad 80
prawn stir-fry 144
prawn toasts 146
sweet potato-topped fish pie 88
prunes: star-of-the-day dessert 208
pumpkin seed & fruit bars 188

quiches: mini quiches 114
red pepper, garlic & Parmesan quiches 114
quinoa: roasted vegetable quinoa with toasted cashews 66

rainbow tart 202
raspberries: fairy crumble 204
hot-pink porridge 18
multicoloured fresh fruit lollies 196
nectarine & raspberry yogurt ice 230
raspberry & orange traybakes 166
spider's web pancakes 216
traffic-light smoothie 234
watermelon & raspberry juice 228
yogurt peach melba lollies 196
rice: butternut squash risotto 106
chicken & pea risotto 106
chicken rice salad 80
prawn rice salad 80
rolls: bread monsters 158
sweet bread roll snacks 158
warm seedy rolls 64
root vegetable bake with nuts & cheese 102
röstis: potato & cheese 86
potato, bacon & tomato 86
rösti with bacon & eggs 92
salmon rösti cakes 92
Rudolph's Santa snacks 162

salads: chicken rice salad 80
chickpea & herb salad 126
prawn rice salad 80
tuna, bean & black olive salad 126
salami, tomato-garlic bread with 54
salmon: salmon goujons 136
salmon pasta bake 82
salmon rösti cakes 92
salsas: cucumber & sweetcorn 146
no-chilli 150
Santa's chocolate snowy snacks 162
sausages: chicken & chorizo pizza 138
morning muffins & tomato ketchup 26
no-mess cheesy pepperoni calzones 116
sausage & beans 24
sausage & pepper burgers 120
sausage & tomato pasties 20
spicy chorizo wrap 74
seeds: crunchy honey yogurt 28
granola squares 174
pumpkin seed & fruit bars 188
warm seedy rolls 64
smoked salmon & asparagus bagels 48
smoothies: breakfast 32
peanut-butter 32
traffic-light 234
snacks 10, 154-93
soups: bean, coconut & spinach 50
red lentil & bacon 50
spaghetti bolognaise 84
Spanish tortilla 112
spider's web pancakes 216
spinach: bean, coconut & spinach soup 50
green cheese pasta 78
spinach & Parmesan twists 168
squash: butternut squash & feta cheese calzones 116
butternut squash risotto 106
mild chicken & squash curry 96
root vegetable bake with nuts & cheese 102
star-of-the-day dessert 208
strawberries: fairy crumble 204
strawberry & vanilla ice cream milkshake 226
strawberry & vanilla milkshake 226
strawberry, banana & cherry pudding 206
strawberry yogurt ice 210

watermelon, pear & strawberry salad 164
white chocolate & strawberry brownies 218
sugar & cinnamon French toast 22
sunset wedges & soured cream 52
sunshine tart 202
supper in a hurry 104
suppers 108-33
sweet & sour pork noodles 144
sweet potatoes: baked sweet potatoes & creamy mushrooms 72
baked sweet potatoes & prawns 72
multicoloured root chips 122
sunset wedges & soured cream 52
sweet potato-topped fish pie 88
sweetcorn: cucumber & sweetcorn salsa 146
sweetcorn fritters & tomato dip 128
tuna pasta bake with sweetcorn 82
tarts: rainbow tart 202
sunshine tart 202
upside-down tarts 186
toast: French toast with blueberries 22
prawn toasts 146
sugar & cinnamon French toast 22
toffee: chocolate-toffee popcorn 180
toffee-apple porridge 18
toffee apples 200
toffee peaches 200
tomatoes: beanfeast 44
herby beans & bacon 24
mini quiches 114
tomato & mushroom muffins 26
tomato dip 128
tomato-garlic bread with ham 54
tomato ketchup 26
tortilla, Spanish 112
tortillas: chicken & bacon wraps 130
chicken fajitas & no-chilli salsa 150
Chinese-style pork & pak choi wraps 62
Chinese-style turkey wraps 62
maple-glazed gammon wraps 56
pan-fried chicken wraps 56
Peking wraps 68
pesto cheese wraps 74
spicy chorizo wrap 74
tuna & coleslaw wraps 130
traffic-light scrambled eggs 40
traffic-light smoothie 234
tuna: cheesy tuna & prawn pie 88
tuna & coleslaw wraps 130
tuna, bean & black olive salad 126
tuna melts 70
tuna pasta bake with sweetcorn 82
turkey wraps, Chinese-style 62

upside-down tarts 186

vanilla & fig pancakes 198
vanilla custard 212
vanilla flowers 184
vegetables: roasted vegetable couscous 66
roasted vegetable quinoa 66
vegetable burgers 120
vegetable hotpot with dumplings 98

watermelon: watermelon & raspberry juice 228
watermelon, pear & strawberry salad 164
wraps *see* tortillas

yogurt: crunchy honey yogurt 28
nectarine & raspberry yogurt ice 230
star-of-the-day dessert 208
strawberry yogurt ice 210
yogurt-coated bars 188
yogurt-coated cereal topping 28
yogurt ice 210
yogurt peach melba lollies 196

acknowledgements

Author's Acknowledgements

Thank you to my sister Sophie for all her help and support during the writing of this book. Also a big thank you to Sophie's and my children for being the tried and trusted recipe testers!

Executive Editor Nicky Hill
Editor Kerenza Swift
Executive Art Editor Mark Stevens
Designer Richard Scott
Photographer Lis Parsons
Home Economist Emma Jane Frost
Props Stylist Liz Hippisley
Production Controller Carolin Stransky

Commissioned Photography © Octopus Publishing Group Ltd/Lis Parsons apart from the following:
© Octopus Publishing Group Limited/Vanessa Davies 8, 11, 12, 115, 158, 163, 169, 185, 191, 193, 225, 228, 233, 235.